IDEAS & HOW-TO

Garden Structures

Meredith® Books
Des Moines, Iowa

Better Homes and Gardens®Ideas and How-To Garden Structures
Editor: Michael McKinley
Contributing Project Manager: Veronica Lorson Fowler
Writer: Bill LaHay
Contributing Graphic Designer: Matthew Eberhart,
  Evil Eye Design, Inc.
Copy Chief: Terri Fredrickson
Copy Editor: Kevin Cox
Publishing Operations Manager: Karen Schirm
Senior Editor, Asset & Information Management: Phillip Morgan
Edit and Design Production Coordinator: Mary Lee Gavin
Art and Editorial Sourcing Coordinator: Kathy Stevens
Editorial Assistant: Susan Ferguson
Book Production Managers: Pam Kvitne, Marjorie J. Schenkelberg,
  Rick von Holdt, Mark Weaver
Imaging Center Operator: Vicki Morlan
Contributing Copy Editor: Susan Lang
Contributing Proofreaders: Pamela Elizian, Jodie Littleton, Stephanie Petersen
Cover Photographer: Stephen Cridland
Contributing Photographer: Page 94, Catriona Tudor Erler
Contributing Indexer: Ellen Sherron
Contributing Illustrator: Chuck Lockhart

Meredith® Books
Editor in Chief: Gregory H. Kayko
Executive Director, Design: Matt Strelecki
Managing Editor: Amy Tincher-Durik
Executive Editor: Benjamin W. Allen
Senior Editor/Group Manager: Vicki Leigh Ingham
Senior Associate Design Director: Ken Carlson
Marketing Product Manager: Brent Wiersma

Executive Director, Marketing and New Business: Kevin Kacere
Editorial Director: Linda Raglan Cunningham
Executive Director, New Business Development: Todd M. Davis
Director, Marketing and Publicity: Amy Nichols
Executive Director, Sales: Ken Zagor
Director, Operations: George A. Susral
Director, Production: Douglas M. Johnston
Business Director: Jim Leonard

Vice President and General Manager: Douglas J. Guendel

Better Homes and Gardens® **Magazine**
Editor in Chief: Gayle Goodson Butler
Deputy Editor, Home Design: Oma Blaise Ford

Meredith Publishing Group
President: Jack Griffin
Senior Vice President: Karla Jeffries

Meredith Corporation
Chairman of the Board: William T. Kerr
President and Chief Executive Officer: Stephen M. Lacy

Garden Structures

All of us at Meredith® Books are dedicated to providing you with information and ideas to enhance your home. We welcome your comments and suggestions. Write to us at: Meredith Books, Home Decorating and Design Editorial Department, 1716 Locust St., Des Moines, IA 50309-3023.

Note to the Readers: Due to differing conditions, tools, and individual skills, Meredith Corporation assumes no responsibility for any damages, injuries suffered, or losses incurred as a result of following the information published in this book. Before beginning any project, review the instructions carefully, and if any doubts or questions remain, consult local experts or authorities. Because codes and regulations vary greatly, you always should check with authorities to ensure that your project complies with all applicable local codes and regulations. Always read and observe all of the safety precautions provided by manufacturers of any tools, equipment, or supplies, and follow all accepted safety procedures.

Contents

Chapter 1: Planning and Design **8**

Designing the Right Garden Structure for You.... 10

Creating Smart Design 12

Making Your Garden Structure Look at Home 14

Garden Structure Benefits................................... 17

Creating Privacy 18

The Right Spot for an Garden Structure 20

Lighting... 26

Winter Interest.. 27

Choosing Materials for Your Garden Structure... 28

Paints and Finishes 38

Garden Structure Kits 42

Construction Primer.. 44

Code Issues 46

Working With Contractors................................... 47

Budgeting Time and Money................................. 48

Chapter 2: Trellises **50**

About Trellises 52

Simple Wall-Mounted Trellises 54

Incorporating Circles 56

Incorporating Curved Tops................................. 58

Designing Wall-Mounted Trellises 60

Freestanding Trellises 63

Trellises as a Privacy Solution 66

Building a Bamboo Trellis................................... 70

Tuteurs and Obelisks 72

Building With Copper 75

Using Found or Repurposed Materials 76

Chapter 3: Arbors **78**

About Arbors 80

Building a Classic Arbor 86

Arbors With Gates 90

Asian-Inspired Arbors 94

Arbors With Seating 98

Arbors as Front Entries......................................102

Arbors With Fences..106

Apertures in Arbors 110

Tunnel Arbors 113

Arbors on Pedestals 116

Creating Curved-Top Arbors..............................118

Rustic Arbors...122

Rustic Construction Techniques 125

Chapter 4: Pergolas 126

About Pergolas 128
A Classic Pergola 132
Attached Pergolas 135
Building Pergolas With Decks 138
Wall-Mounted Pergolas Above Doorways 142
Freestanding Pergolas 144
Pergolas With Fences and Trellises 146
Corner Pergolas 149
Pergolas with Curved Tops 150
Pergolas for Dining 153
Pergolas With Outdoor Kitchens 154
Rustic Pergolas 156

Chapter 5: Gazebos 158

About Gazebos 160
Gazebos From Kits 164
Gazebos as Part of Decks and Porches 166
Gazebo Construction 169
Gazebo Roofs 172
Rustic Gazebos 176

Chapter 6: Pavilions and Other Structures . 178

About Pavilions 180
Ramadas 186
Screened Spaces 188
Teahouses 192
Incorporating Fabric 194
Garden Structures With Fireplaces 196
Porticos and Entries 199
Lath Houses 202
Side Yard Solutions 204
Whimsical Garden Structures 210
Vines for Garden Structures 212

Glossary 221
Index 222

Introduction

Often called the "bones of a garden," garden structures and other hardscape immediately and distinctively add character and function to a landscape.

Case in point: A pretty backyard with lots of plantings is one thing, but a pretty backyard with a long pergola stretching across the back, blocking problematic views and draped in, say, wisteria with seating underneath is quite another.

In this book you'll not only get many ideas for garden structures, you'll also be walked through the process of deciding what type of garden structure will work best for you and your landscape.

The first chapter of the book is devoted to planning and design, a critical step since a garden structure is large and likely to be around for decades.

You'll get basic planning and siting tips, as well as ideas on how to use a garden structure to solve landscape problems such as privacy, utilizing limited space, adding winter interest, and taming slopes.

You'll also be walked through choosing the best materials for your structure, as well as appropriate finishes, lighting, and the basic construction techniques involved.

As you read through this book, you'll notice that this is not a highly detailed construction how-to book that takes you from the first cut of a board through the last flick of a paintbrush.

Instead this book is aimed at the accomplished do-it-yourselfer or at the homeowner who has some great ideas, but limited expertise and time, and will be hiring a contractor or working with highly skilled friends and family to tackle a large garden structure project.

In this book you'll see information and construction details on the most popular garden structures.

Throughout you'll find plenty of beautiful photos with classic and innovative structures alike. Combined with rundowns on basic planning and an overview of construction techniques, they're sure to set you on the path to the perfect garden structure for you.

This storybook arbor is the perfect portal to connect two garden rooms or to put at the back of a garden for visitors to leave or enter through.

This lightweight pavilion, covered with bamboo slatting, creates just enough shade and a sense of enclosure to make a perfect nook for relaxing.

1 Planning and

When you embark on any building venture, you face a range of possible designs and details that can make even a modest project intimidating. The good news is that garden structures can be among the most straightforward to construct.

This chapter offers a variety of ideas on garden structure design and on the best ways to tackle a project, whether as a do-it-yourselfer, with help from family and friends, or by hiring it out to a contractor.

Of course the larger the structure and the more complex its design, the more care you'll need to put into it. But build the structure well and you'll enjoy it for many years.

After all, garden structures are about enjoyment. They help shape the character of a garden, provide a place to relax with friends on a weekend, or create a beautiful spot to wind down after a hectic day.

Design

Designing the Right Garden Structure for You

When dreaming about the right structure, don't be afraid to think big. Imagining costs nothing and sometimes you can come up with more creative solutions and alternatives than you ever would if you consciously limited yourself by thinking first about time and money.

Gather all the ideas you can. This book is a great start, but also tear out pages from magazines and take a digital camera or sketch pad on garden tours and to public gardens. As you examine your collection of images, you'll find similar traits that will help you determine what you want.

Most of your best imagining will be done standing or sitting in your landscape. Envision not only the placement of various structures but also how you and others might use and enjoy them. Keep in mind that many landscapes can accommodate multiple structures. Do you want something just to give definition to the landscape, or to serve as an outdoor shelter or activity center? Is one particular spot in the yard just crying out for a strong focal point? Is privacy a concern? What have you seen elsewhere that you'd love to translate to your own landscape?

As you ponder these questions, your focus will sharpen and you'll be able to select more easily from among the basic structure types described in this book—trellis, arbor, pergola, gazebo, or pavilion.

You'll also have a firmer idea about how you want that structure to function and how you want it constructed.

This vibrant arbor works more as an outdoor sculpture than a highly functional structure, adding year-round height and color. Once the small vines planted at its feet mature, it will also be an excellent habitat for birds.

This pergola has classic rounded columns and beautifully detailed crossbeams that pick up on architectural details from the house. Underlaid with slate pavers and wired with ceiling fans, it's a gorgeous spot for a meal morning, noon, or night.

This arbor succeeds beautifully in part because it so closely mimics the Arts and Crafts style of the home. It also manages to draw people into an otherwise little-used side yard and adds curb appeal to the home. It's also a good example of how substantial a garden structure can be. This one boasts stone pedestals and hefty tapered columns.

❧ Creating Smart Design

When designing a garden structure, there are amazingly few rules. Aside from the limitations of local building codes or city ordinances, the main thing is that the structure be well made and sound to give it adequate substance in the landscape, prevent it from tilting or swaying, and make sure it's safe.

For all but the smallest structures, it's probably smart to invest in the services of a professional designer who will bring to the project an eye for proportion, scale, balance, and design that a builder might lack. If your builder's point of pride is graceful or innovative design, you may want to give that person a go—but ask for a scale drawing first.

This summerhouse may have mere lath for walls, but it's a substantial, well-planned structure with a well-designed shake roof. The floor is raised slightly to make sure it's high and dry in all types of weather and with electricity for lighting, it can be enjoyed well into the night. The light blue ceiling inside creates a delightful, airy visual surprise.

DESIGN DOS AND DON'TS

Do:

- Take design cues from favorite details on your home's exterior.
- Mix two or three materials or colors for more interest.
- Develop the structure's design as part of a master plan for the site.
- Include spaces for plants and other landscape features such as decks, patios, sidewalks, fences, and garages.
- Consider the backdrop. What will be behind the structure and how will it affect your view of the structure? And remember that the backdrop is more than just 6 feet high—it could be 16 or 60 feet high if you can see that space.

Don't:

- Disregard prominent stylistic/regional influences (see page 14).
- Work against the site. Build into a sloping site, if practical, rather than trying to level it. Work with the openness of a flat site rather than trying to create large berms or slopes.
- Build something so large it overwhelms or crowds its surroundings or so small that it's dwarfed by its surroundings. Strive for appropriate scale.
- Mix so many materials or colors that the result looks chaotic.
- Forget to consider prevailing winds and seasonal sun location.

Without this massive pergola, this corner of the yard would have been a nothing space. Now, the hefty structure adds height and presence to the corner, creating a focal point and an anchor for the seating underneath and around it. Its solid design echos the Arts and Crafts design of the fence behind it, and the little bit of color in the wood atop the stone pedestal helps blend it with the stone and pavers.

Making Your Garden Structure Look at Home

Whether you are sketching project ideas yourself or hiring a design professional, keep one goal foremost in mind: Your finished structure should look as if it belongs in its spot.

This is especially true for any structures that are attached or adjacent to your home, garage, or outbuildings. You don't need to produce a carbon copy. Just add recognizable elements that create the suggestion of a family resemblance, the way siblings might share some features or mannerisms.

Repeating colors, materials, and architectural features is the simplest way to ensure this connection, and it might include aiming for compatibility with neighboring homes as well. If your home is brick, consider brick paving around the structure. If your home is light gray, try painting the garden structure the same hue. To complement a home with shake siding, use a shake roof on the structure. (Keep in mind that communities have regulations that restrict designs and require approval from a governing board.)

Taking regional style into account is also important. An Asian arbor, for example, crafted from mahogany or another exotic wood would look odd tucked into a neighborhood of white Cape Cod homes.

The more detailing on a home's exterior, the easier it is to introduce similar complexity to an outdoor structure. This pergola's turned ornamental posts, scrollwork frieze, and lattice roof mimic the textured and ornate surfaces found on this Victorian-style home.

The portico framing this home's front entry blends seamlessly with its setting. Subtle though it may be, the portico creates a shelted space that beckons visitors and gives the unusually placed front door more prominence.

The matching color is the most obvious element tying this pergola to its Arts and Crafts bungalow, but it's not the only one. The stepped horizontal braces and interconnected timbers are a trademark Craftsman touch, which helps the structure look more at home with the Craftsman home.

Previously there was no real place to enjoy the shade and seclusion provided by the trees. A gazebo solved that problem by creating a destination for relaxing. A brick patio leads to the gazebo and is also a great space for entertaining large groups.

Garden Structure Benefits

Garden structures aren't just nice to look at. They also can serve several practical purposes.

A garden structure provides a focal point for the landscape. Outdoor spaces are more pleasing when there's a clear focal point in view. It can be as simple as a bench or fountain, or as large and complex as a gazebo or pergola.

A garden structure also provides living space. Depending on the type of structure you build, it can be a wonderful extension of your home, housing a dining area, space for relaxing, or even a fireplace, fire pit, or outdoor kitchen.

And it provides privacy. Trellises, latticed screens, and the vines that grow on them allow you to enjoy your yard better by blocking views from neighbors or passersby. They also allow you to not have to view the outside world, providing a sense of enclosure.

A garden structure provides shade. Depending on the type of roof on your structure, you can cool outdoor areas for your own enjoyment, prevent indoor heat gain by shading windows, or protect favorite plants.

As this pergola illustrates, the suggestion of shelter is sometimes an effective substitute for actual walls and a roof. By defining this patio area, the pergola and planters create the effect of an outdoor room. The overhead framing also provides welcome shade for the large windows.

Creating Privacy

Garden structures lend themselves well to creating privacy. Trellises are the most efficient at the task, but even an arbor (which is basically an outdoor doorway) can screen a view if a tall fence stretches from either side of it.

Many homeowners rely on vines covering their outdoor structures to screen views. However in many climates vines have leaves only a few months of the year, leaving the space somewhat stark the remainder of the time, including early spring when you most want to get out into your yard and enjoy the newly balmy weather.

It also takes a few years for perennial vines to truly blanket a structure. Annuals mature faster but often don't get large until at least late summer, so they don't provide privacy for months after you've planted the seeds or seedlings.

An alternative solution is to plant evergreen shrubs or trees alongside or around a structure. The structure provides partial privacy the first year or two and the plants provide more and more privacy each year as they grow. And because they're evergreens they filter views year-round.

IDEAS FOR CREATING PRIVACY

- As much as possible rely on the structure itself to provide personal space. Vines add a layer of privacy and soften the structure visually, but they may not be able to do it all year long.
- Use lattice with caution. Those latticework panels are great timesavers, but don't use them in great unbroken expanses or the effect will be confining. Break up the panels by framing them with lengths of lumber or by creating windowlike openings in the lattice. (See pages 56 and 111.)
- Consider views from higher up. If you have neighbors with houses two stories or higher, take into account views from upper-story windows. A slatted or other type of overhead structure will allow you to enjoy your yard in privacy.
- Don't forget fabric. A structure can provide part of the privacy, and expanses of fabric can further screen views. (See page 194.)
- Don't create a privacy problem. Try to design a deck or patio to be low rather than high. A high seating area puts you on display much more than a lower one, and only the most extensive trellising system will block views.

This trellised screen wraps around the patio, making it distinctively different and also adding an attractive curve that envelops anyone relaxing near it. It incorporates small "windows" along the top so that views outward aren't obstructed completely, keeping an open, friendly feeling.

A series of large-grid panels cap built-in benches wrapped around the edge of this spectacular deck, creating a private setting perfect for conversation or just relaxing. The deck's position on a steep hillside also ensures more privacy since the rough terrain precludes passersby or neighbors being able to see in.

The Right Spot for a Garden Structure

The goal of placing a garden structure should be to make it look as though it's in the perfect spot.

In a smaller yard the choices are limited, but even then, think creatively. If you want a pergola, you don't have to place it right next to the house. Perhaps it would be better positioned as a destination to draw people into the landscape.

The play between sun and shade in your yard is important. Because many large garden structures are built to provide shade, it's important that you understand how shade varies according to sun position throughout the seasons.

Also consider how windy a site is. Wind can make a spot unpleasant and over time can uproot all but the best-built structures.

And remember outbuildings, trees, or water features. They must work together with the structure. Also think about future features you might add and how the structure would work with them.

Small urban yards offer limited options for outdoor structures, but that doesn't necessarily mean radical downsizing works best. This charming lath house proves a tight fit on this patio, but it creates a cozy dining area that makes the tiny yard feel more functional. The peaked roof is a smart feature that screens the neighbor's garage and home.

Built to define a conversation area in a small formal garden, this simple pergola benefits from being tucked into a niche near the fence and away from the house.

TIPS FOR CHOOSING THE RIGHT SITE

- Measure the available yard area and draw a scaled plan on paper. As an alternative mark the footprint of the structure with landscaping spray paint or string and stakes to make sure it feels right in three dimensions.
- Check with local building officials to see what codes or ordinances apply, such as a minimum required setback from property lines.
- Keep track of sun and shade patterns for several weeks or even months, so you can gauge the exposure for a particular spot.
- Make sure water runoff can be diverted around the structure.
- With a structure for entertaining or an outdoor kitchen, stay close to the house for access to electrical and plumbing lines.
- When working around trees or other large plants, leave enough room to allow for their mature canopy and root system. As a rule the roots of trees stretch out as far as their branches and shouldn't be disturbed or built over.

The Right Spot for a Garden Structure

BUILDING ON A SLOPE

Few building sites are perfectly flat and level, though some feature a mild grade that allows for a slab foundation or only slight adjustments for independent footings. However sloped terrain may be unavoidable or, in some cases, may offer the best placement for a structure because of better views, space limitations, or other factors.

Varying terrain offers opportunities for something dramatic, but it's essential that they're well engineered to ensure good water drainage and to prevent shifting soil that weakens the structure. The steeper the slope, the more gravity will force soil and water against the structural foundations.

This Asian-style structure negotiates its sloped perch with the help of separate offset pier footings and downhill posts that extend well below the floor framing. This method provides a simpler solution than trying to terrace such a steep site and makes water runoff easier to manage. The floor platform is cantilevered beyond the posts.

SLOPE SOLUTIONS

Here are four of the most common ways to build the floor of a structure into a slope.

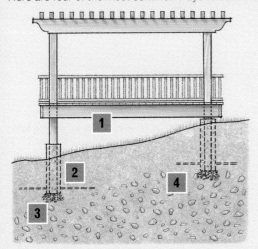

Offset Pier Footings allow some height discrepancies for the bottom ends of posts. You can compensate for the differences when the floor deck or roof frame is added. As long as the footings are sufficiently deep, they provide stable support.
1. Floor platform
2. Posts embedded in concrete pier footings
3. Crushed rock for drainage
4. Frost line (posts go below that depth)

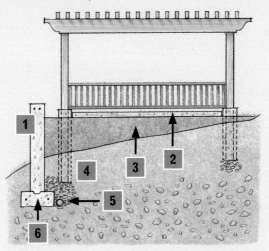

Fill Terracing involves building a retaining wall downhill from the structure, then adding soil for a level pad. Proper compaction of fill is essential. Crushed rock is placed behind the wall for drainage. The downhill pier penetrates the fill into undisturbed soil.
1. Concrete retaining wall
2. Slab or pavers
3. Compacted fill dirt
4. Pier footings in undisturbed soil
5. Drain running under wall, out to daylight
6. Reinforced concrete continuous footing

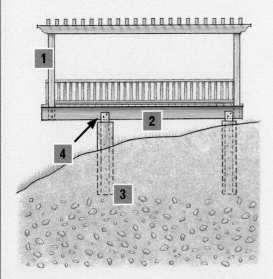

Cantilevered construction relies on solid anchoring for the uphill portion of the structure so the downhill end can extend into the air as if floating. This technique often requires some complex engineering for the footings and for the structural frame cantilevered from them, so professional design help is a must.
1. Railings for safety
2. Cantilevered floor frame
3. Reinforced concrete pier footings
4. Beams bolted to piers

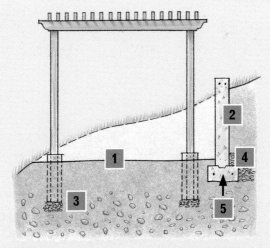

Excavation Terracing reverses the fill strategy but yields a similar result. Soil is removed to create a level building pad, and a retaining wall holds back the soil on the uphill side of the structure. This method relies mostly on undisturbed soil for support and requires a well-built retaining wall with good drainage behind it.
1. Soil removed to create level floor area
2. Concrete retaining wall
3. Posts embedded in concrete pier footings
4. Drain leading to daylight (or weep holes in retaining wall)
5. Reinforced concrete continuous footing

The Right Spot for a Garden Structure

PREPARING THE SITE

In the same way that a tree needs soil-clutching roots to keep it upright and steady, a garden structure needs a solid connection to the earth.

A proper foundation anchors the structure so winds or other forces don't move or upend it, and also prevents unwanted or uneven settling into the ground. Typically a masonry foundation serves as the anchor. It is often made of poured-in-place concrete but sometimes of brick, concrete block, or stone. In regions where frost heave occurs in winter, a foundation provides added stability by allowing the entire structure to "float" as one unit (on a concrete slab base) or by penetrating deep enough into the soil (via pier footings) to remain unaffected by the surface movement of the freezing and thawing soil.

Metal hardware, coated to resist corrosion from the elements, ties wood or metal posts, beams, and other framing members to the foundation. Some structures feature a paver base or slab floor that is independent of the rest of the structure.

Various structures need different supports. The more top-heavy the structure, the more likely it will require multiple posts embedded deep into the ground, preferably in concrete pier footings. Pergolas are the best example, but even smaller structures such as trellises may need deep concrete footings, especially if they have only two posts and feature large flat surfaces that tend to get pushed around by wind gusts. Keep in mind also that the structure might have two or more "bases" that function independently. For example, a pergola might feature individual concrete pier footings to support the structure itself, plus a center patio base of brick pavers on sand. A concrete slab base can sometimes function as both the floor and a structural foundation, but any area that supports posts directly should be at least 12 inches thick and reinforced with steel rebar to help prevent cracking.

BUILDING A BASE FOR AN OUTDOOR STRUCTURE

There are two basic ways to provide a base for an outdoor structure. A concrete slab is the most sturdy and when set high enough provides the driest surface. But in many cases, where perfectly flat surfaces and durability aren't critical, brick or pavers set into sand will do nicely as well.

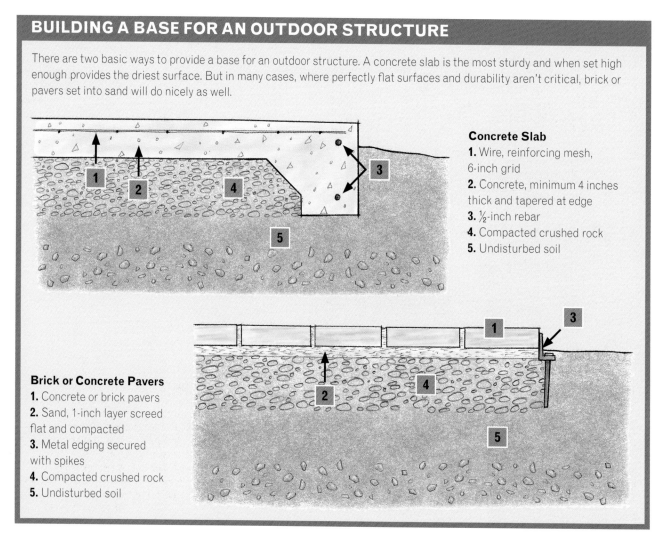

Concrete Slab
1. Wire, reinforcing mesh, 6-inch grid
2. Concrete, minimum 4 inches thick and tapered at edge
3. $\frac{1}{2}$-inch rebar
4. Compacted crushed rock
5. Undisturbed soil

Brick or Concrete Pavers
1. Concrete or brick pavers
2. Sand, 1-inch layer screed flat and compacted
3. Metal edging secured with spikes
4. Compacted crushed rock
5. Undisturbed soil

ANCHORING THE POSTS

These are the three most common ways to secure posts into soil.

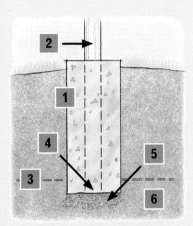 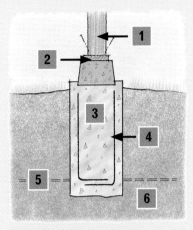 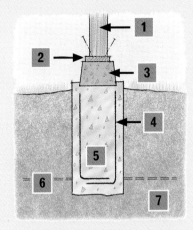

Embedded in Concrete Pier
This type of post anchoring is ideal for freestanding structures because it can take heavy lateral and vertical loads. It's slightly more expensive than the other options, and the wood in the ground is prone to rot eventually.
1. Concrete post (12-inch diameter)
2. Pressure-treated wood post, the most rot-resistant kind of wood
3. Frost line
4. Post extends to end of concrete pier
5. Compressed crushed rock, 3-inch layer
6. Undisturbed soil

Bolted to Pier Bracket
Suitable for freestanding structures with four or more posts, this option handles moderate lateral loads. Since the post is above ground, it's less likely to rot, and if the structure settles the post can be more easily replaced to make up for the settling.
1. Cedar or pressure-treated post
2. $\frac{1}{2}$-inch bolts through metal post base bracket set into wet concrete
3. Concrete pier footing, minimum 10 inches in diameter
4. $\frac{1}{2}$-inch steel rebar
5. Frost line
6. Undisturbed soil

Precast Pier with Wood Block
This option is fast and inexpensive, but its resistance to lateral loads is relatively weak. It is acceptable for structures that will be attached to a building.
1. Cedar or pressure-treated post
2. Screws or nails toenailed through post into wood block below
3. Precast concrete pier set into footing
4. $\frac{1}{2}$-inch steel rebar
5. Concrete footing, 12-inch diameter
6. Frost line
7. Undisturbed soil

Though it has a heavy timber frame and the adjacent buildings offer some protection from strong winds, this portico still requires solid anchoring to the ground. The concrete patio below is stable but not thick enough to bear the weight of the clustered posts, so independent pier footings penetrate the slab to provide direct support. The raised piers also keep the post ends drier, preventing decay.

Lighting

Add lighting to your outdoor structure and you'll be able to enjoy your garden getaway for many hours longer every day.

Even when you're not actually in the structure, outdoor lighting can make it a striking focal point in your landscape well after dark. Candles and lanterns are always an option, but for light bright enough to actually see your dinner, you'll need electrical light.

If the structure is close to your house, adding direct wiring is usually highly affordable. The cost will be higher if it's farther out, but depending on the structure, may make up a tiny fraction of the overall budget.

A low-cost alternative is low-voltage or solar-powered landscape lighting, either of which is fairly inexpensive and easy to do yourself.

Low-voltage landscape lighting converts your home's 110-volt current into a safer 12 volts. The cable doesn't have to be buried or contained in conduit like standard wiring. For even simpler installation, opt for solar powered fixtures. Newer versions feature bright LED (light-emitting diode) lamps and more efficient photo voltaic panels, though illumination levels still can't rival direct-wired systems that use standard or low-voltage current.

Most outdoor lighting looks better when it's less intense. This simple lantern is direct-wired and could be equipped to give off a much brighter light, but the softer effect from a low-wattage bulb works better for lighting a garden.

Sturdy vertical posts are an excellent support for hanging exterior lights, such as this one. Just run the wire up the post.

OUTDOOR LIGHTING OPTIONS

- Get creative. Don't settle for just a single light overhead. Think about ambient and overhead task lighting or sconces mounted on either side of an entry or along the perimeter of the structure. Exterior grade Christmas lights in interesting shapes or colors can add a festive touch.
- Consider uplights, which add nighttime drama to the structure's architecture.
- Use solar or low-voltage path lights to illuminate walkways for visual drama and also for safety.
- Light nearby trees and walls from below with landscape lights for a more dramatic look.
- Place candles, hanging lanterns, and torches in glass surrounds for safety, and never leave them unattended.

Winter Interest

In regions that see a dramatic change in temperatures and weather conditions from summer to winter, outdoor structures such as pergolas and gazebos typically don't see year-round use. Still they can continue to function as attractive landscape elements, a sort of practical sculpture.

Lighting is one of the simplest features for adding enjoyment to a structure throughout the year, especially if reflections off the snow work to enhance the landscape. Beyond that role, structures must be able to endure the harsh weather and emerge intact when spring arrives.

Even if you aren't concerned about winter aesthetics, plan your structure to withstand winter. Make sure that roof components, lattice panels, and other parts can handle the added weight from a severe ice storm or snowstorm and allow for thorough drainage of water that lands on floors and other horizontal surfaces.

Snow and chilly weather might discourage active use of most garden structures, but this classic arbor works as a wonderful landscape feature even when it's idle.

PLANNING FOR WINTER APPEAL

Nearly any garden structure topped with snow will look lovely in cold weather. There are some things you can do to maximize the effect:

- Position the structure where you can see it clearly from inside the house, the main vantage point in cold weather.
- When landscaping around the structure, use evergreens to soften the look of the structure year round. In regions where temperatures seldom dip below 20°F/-7°C, plant evergreens in containers. (In colder regions the soil freezes solid in the containers and kills the plants.)
- As you design the structure, keep in mind opportunities to hang wreaths, garlands, and other seasonal greens.
- Consider a power source so that you can easily install holiday lighting.

Choosing Materials for Your Garden Structure

The materials you use to construct an arbor, gazebo, or other structure are an integral part of the design, engineering, and sometimes even the function.

Brick, natural stone, metal, and many other materials are used to build garden structures, but none are used as widely as wood. And for good reason. Wood is versatile, easy to work, readily available, relatively lightweight, and often much less expensive than other building materials.

But wood is not perfect. It can rot, crack, and burn, and it requires finishing materials such as paints and stains to help it last longer outdoors. Even with those drawbacks wood is still a wise choice for many garden structures.

The advantages and disadvantages of four species commonly used for exterior projects are described below, but those four woods don't represent all the options. Other worthy choices are teak, mahogany, cypress, yellow cedar, white oak, and locust—but they are expensive and harder to come by in large sizes (they may have to be special ordered). Among the woods to avoid for outdoor structures are red oak, maple, birch, beech, poplar, and untreated pine. These species all have poor resistance to insects and to fungi that thrive when wood is constantly exposed to humidity, rain, and other precipitation.

RECOMMENDED LUMBER FOR OUTDOOR STRUCTURES

Pressure-Treated Yellow Pine	Western Red Cedar	Redwood	Ipe
• Originates in southern United States	• Originates in Canada, U.S. Pacific Northwest	• Originates in California, Oregon	• Originates in Brazil (pronounced EE-pay)
• Economical	• More expensive than yellow pine but still fairly affordable	• More expensive than pine or cedar	• Fairly expensive
• Chemically treated for high resistance to rot and insects	• Good natural resistance to rot and insects	• Heartwood has good natural resistance to rot and insects	• Excellent resistance to rot, insects, and fire
• Offered in many sizes, including 6×6 and larger timbers	• Offered in many sizes, including 6×6 timbers	• Offered in limited sizes	• Offered in limited sizes; used mainly for decks
• Holds stains and sealers well but not suitable for painting	• Excellent for stains, sealers, and most paints	• Excellent for stains, sealers, and most paints	• Finish with clear sealers or penetrating oils
• Widely available	• Nationwide in-stock availability	• Mostly West Coast availability; some environmental issues	• Limited availability
• Moderately heavy, durable; needs finish for best look	• Lightweight, but dents and burns easily	• Lightweight, but dents easily; good fire resistance	• Very heavy and durable, but hard to work

Most outdoor structures feature a mix of materials, as is true of this pergola. Its cedar overhead framework, left to weather naturally, sits atop painted architectural columns. (Most columns used outdoors are made of fiberglass for better durability.) Supporting the structure are pedestal walls constructed of natural stone and topped with concrete capstones.

Choosing Materials for Your Garden Structure

LIVE BRANCH

This method is often referred to as rustic (though other rough or naturalistic styles are also sometimes called rustic). The term live branch is more specific and refers to branches and logs that are used in their natural state, without cutting them straight or smooth like conventional lumber. The branches may or may not have bark on them, depending on the species and when it was harvested. Simple notched or butt joinery with large spikes or screws is the common way to assemble the components. Left unfinished and natural, the branches tend to attract insects and will likely have a shorter life span than milled and sealed lumber. This material can create a lighthearted, whimsical, or even primitive look.

ROUGH-SAWN LUMBER

Also called rough-hewn, this is simply stock that has been cut to rough size but not dressed smooth by a planer or molder. The material dominated construction methods for more than a century after water-powered sawmills became numerous enough to produce large quantities of it. Today most lumber is milled smooth, but salvaged or reclaimed wood from old barns and other buildings often has the trademark splintery surface that is evidence of a circular or bandsaw blade. A close cousin, rough-hewn lumber is milled by hand with adzes, broadaxes, and drawknives, yielding a chiseled surface with visible tool marks. Both types are considered rustic or historic.

BRICK, STONE, AND CONCRETE

They rarely account for all or even most of a garden structure, but masonry materials offer two very significant advantages over wood—they don't burn and they don't rot. Their rigidity can result in cracking, and mortar joints can degrade over time, but under normal conditions deterioration takes nearly a century. In the meantime these materials serve as foundations, footings, pedestals, columns, and other critical architectural features. The combined costs of premium materials and labor-intensive craftsmanship make masonry structures fairly expensive, but when initial cost is weighed against longevity the investment is a bargain.

With its masonry base, natural log posts, and elaborate roof trusses, this rustic pavilion offers a good example of how seemingly disparate materials can be combined successfully. The informality of such structures makes it easier to establish an eclectic theme throughout an entire garden, mixing a variety of plants and decorative objects.

Although live-branch structures are often small and simple, there's no reason more ambitious projects cannot incorporate this type of material, as long as the joinery is sound. This pergola features log and branch sections large enough to function as structural timbers.

Choosing Materials for Your Garden Structure

COPPER

Although copper is distinctive, durable, and easy to work, its relatively high cost makes it better suited to smaller projects or as an accent. It's widely available and most affordable in three common forms—solid bare wire, flexible tubing, and rigid pipe. The wire is a cinch to cut, twist, and wrap, while the tubing and pipe can be cut with common plumbing tools. Exposed copper eventually develops a brown patina that later turns a mottled green.

SALVAGE AND VINTAGE

Pieces suitable for garden structures are often but not exclusively made of metal, probably because the only competition comes from wood, which tends to decay outdoors. Good salvage pieces can range from weathered wrought-iron fencing to a brass headboard, a mahogany ship's wheel, or an old cast-iron vent register. These items are especially useful as accents or as trellises since they offer climbing plants plenty of opportunity to take hold. There's a lot of demand for unusual "character" pieces.

BAMBOO

A natural choice for any design with an Asian flavor, bamboo is technically a grass but like wood comes in a variety of species with different looks and characteristics. Garden centers often stock smaller sizes (up to 1 inch diameter) of one or two common varieties, but for exotic versions or bigger diameters try an online search as well as specialty vendors. Bamboo is strong but brittle when dry, so mechanical fasteners such as nails and screws tend to split it if you don't drill first. For better results and a more authentic look, tie joints together with twine or reeds.

Choosing Materials for Your Garden Structure

OTHER METAL

Other metals, such as steel and iron, may not be quite as easy to work as wood but are striking in the garden.

First metal is a hardworking material. A timber post or beam might have to be massive to be strong, but wrought iron, steel, and aluminum can substitute in a much lighter-looking form. A metal with various embellisments also keeps that detail in a way wood can't (the details often break or wear away over the years). These traits make metal a great option for creating a finer or more graceful look than you'll be able to get from wood or masonry.

And except for unprotected steel or iron in an oceanfront environment, metal typically lasts longer than wood.

Done well, however, metal design and fabrication require specialized tools and techniques that aren't as plentiful as the basic carpentry skills most contractors can offer. Check phone book listings under "Ornamental iron work" or "Metal fabrication" and explain that rather than industrial fabrication (the most common jobs for such places) you want decorative residential work and may need design assistance.

This long arbor offers a good example of how light the scale of a metal structure can be. Designed as a simple framework, it will almost disappear completely as the vines on it continue to grow and mature. If fashioned from wood, the arbor would sport heavy posts and thick arches that would lack the open feeling of this version.

This metal arbor adds interest and height to this open patio area and better defines and encloses the space to make it more cozy for dining.

Choosing Materials for Your Garden Structure

WIRE AND MESH

Less commonly incorporated into outdoor garden structures, wire and mesh deserve much greater use. They're durable and can be used endlessly in creative ways that add function and style to a structure.

Wire can be as small as the fine aluminum screen fabric used to deter insects. More heavy-duty is hardware cloth, typically fashioned with ¼- to ½-inch grids. Steel grid mesh, which has squares up to 6 inches across, is heavier still; it is normally used to reinforce concrete slabs.

Other woven metal fabrics such as chicken wire feature lightweight wire arranged to create hexagonal openings 1 or 2 inches across. Any of these larger mesh fabrics can function as trellis materials for climbing plants, but most aren't stout enough to stand sturdily without some help. Metal or wood frames are usually required for support.

The open weave of wire fabrics creates interesting visual textures but not much privacy. Sheets of perforated metals, especially aluminum, work better for that purpose.

Repurposing materials for use in a garden structure is part of the fun in creating the structure. Here a pergola set up for outdoor dining is fitted with a heavy steel mesh designed for reinforcing concrete slabs. The mesh will support climbing plants if desired, but left bare it creates an illusion of paned windows.

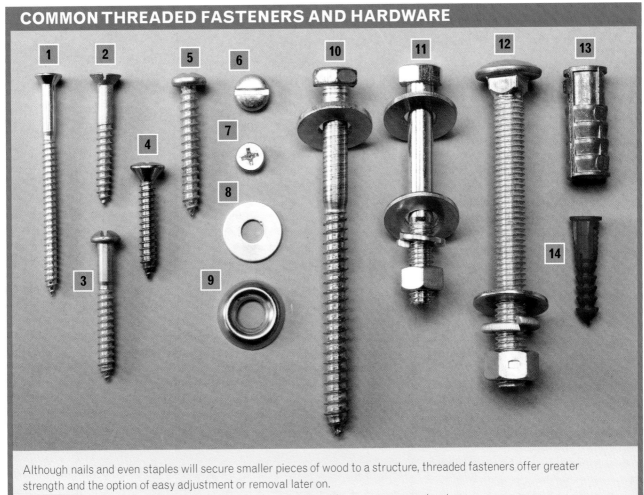

COMMON THREADED FASTENERS AND HARDWARE

Although nails and even staples will secure smaller pieces of wood to a structure, threaded fasteners offer greater strength and the option of easy adjustment or removal later on.

The most commonly available types are shown here along with some accessory hardware.

1. Flathead wood screw (Phillips drive)
2. Flathead wood screw (slot drive)
3. Roundhead wood screw (slot drive)
4. Ovalhead sheet metal screw
5. Panhead sheet metal screw
6. Slot-drive screw head
7. Phillips-drive screw head
8. Flat washer
9. Finishing washer
10. Lag screw, with flat washer
11. Hex-head bolt (or cap screw), with washers and hex nut
12. Carriage bolt, with washers and hex nut
13. Lag shield (lead)
14. Expansion anchor (plastic)

HARDWARE AND FASTENERS

Understanding the various types of hardware and fasteners used in garden structures will help you make intelligent choices in building your project. The result will be a structure that remains sturdy for many years.

The larger parts of structures are typically secured by bolts, lag or timber screws, and sometimes metal brackets that reinforce the connections. For large garden structures, bolt or screw diameters from ¼ to ¾ inch are common, and some specialized fasteners are designed to connect dissimilar materials such as concrete and wood. The best grades for outdoor use are galvanized, hot dipped (coated with a thick layer of zinc), or stainless steel. These types fare best in all weather and resist corrosion from the chemicals present in pressure-treated and cedar lumber.

The smaller parts of structures typically are attached with screws, nails, or staples. Screws offer the benefit of low-impact installation (no beating things up with hammer blows) and easy removal for future repairs or refinishing. Many contractors also use pneumatic (air-driven) nailers and staplers for their speed and convenience. Like hand-driven nails, these fasteners are difficult to remove without damaging the wood.

Paints and Finishes

NATURAL FINISHES

Nearly all wood structures need protection in the form of a stain or finish. Even wood that has good natural resistance to moisture, insects, and other threats is susceptible to damage from the elements—even from something as seemingly benign as sunshine. The sun exposes wood to ultraviolet (UV) light that eventually transforms all wood species—however light or dark they may be originally—to a muted gray.

Unprotected wood retains moisture, providing an ideal breeding ground for fungi and other destructive organisms. Even if the wood dries out occasionally, the random shrinking (and eventual reswelling) tends to produce cracks and other defects that over time compromise the wood's strength and solidity.

Plan on applying and maintaining a protective finish—unless you want a weathered or rustic look and are not concerned about the structure's longevity. In that case you can simply leave the wood unfinished and let time and nature do its work unfettered.

Although protecting the wood is crucial to most people, completely sealing it off from outside elements is a nice theoretical goal but not really practical or effective. Multiple heavy coats of paint aren't the solution—they'll peel and crack—and such treatments mask the natural color and grain patterns of the wood in a way you may find unacceptable. If keeping those warm wood tones and patterns visible is important to you, use a clear or translucent finish.

Penetrating oils and semitransparent stains offer the simplest solution and the easiest maintenance because they can be renewed simply by applying additional coats. However these stains typically allow some water to penetrate. Exterior-grade top-coat finishes such as alkyd or polyurethane varnishes offer better moisture protection, but they eventually degrade in ultraviolet light and will discolor, crack, and peel, requiring regular upkeep.

Applying a finish with natural wood tones allows a structure to blend more easily into its surroundings. Here a brown semitransparent stain borrows some color from the lumber itself and makes the structure seem a more integral part of the landscape. Paint would accomplish the same visual result but would require much more maintenance.

Vivid wood tones are best achieved with either a very light semitransparent stain or a clear sealer. Staining provides a more consistent color that holds up longer and is easier to replicate with renewal coats when necessary. A clear sealer creates a more dramatic look at first, but it doesn't retard graying and color loss as effectively and it makes recovering the intense tone nearly impossible later on.

TYPE OF FINISH	PROS	CONS
Clear Penetrating Finish Includes oil-varnish blends, wood sealers	Easy to apply; minimal surface prep required for additional treatments. Brings out inherent color in new lumber.	Minimal protection against water and UV rays. Most require petroleum-base solvents or turpentine for cleanup. Can darken over time. Doesn't prevent graying of wood.
Semitransparent Stain Includes oil-base and acrylic/ latex (water-base) formulas	Easy to apply; minimal surface prep required for additional treatments. Supplies color without completely masking wood grain; adds color uniformity to blend different boards or lumber species. Retards graying of wood. Wide range of color choices.	Difficult to get completely natural-looking color since stain pigment tends to override wood tone. Typically allows some water penetration as it ages.
Clear Top-Coat Finish Includes spar/marine varnish, polyurethane varnish, oil/alkyd varnish, water-base varnish	Allows built-up finish with greater depth and more sheen options, including high-gloss. Exterior grades contain UV blockers to retard graying of wood, while intact finish film provides good layer of protection against water penetration, keeping wood stable.	Initial application requires at least two coats (one thinned, one full strength). Oil-base versions require petroleum-base solvents for cleanup. Tends to harden and lose flexibility over time, resulting in surface cracks and then rapid degradation. Tedious prep work required to restore old finish (removing and recoating).

These twin arbors take on a whimsical air with their spirited color scheme, vibrant enough to match the showy flowers. Use bold colors, which dominate a scene, carefully and only on those structures you want to get plenty of attention.

Paints and Finishes

COLOR FINISHES

Color can make an outdoor structure really pop visually, giving your landscape pizzazz. You can use two basic methods to add color to outdoor wood structures: regular paints, which are opaque (no transparency), and stains, which allow some of the grain to show.

For the widest variety of colors on a wood structure, consider an opaque finish. Traditionally this type of finish was available only in exterior-grade oil-base enamel but now it's also available in acrylic/latex paints.

Oil-base paints have the advantage of intensity of color, several sheen options, and great durability. However when you apply oil-base paint to wood, it has to endure wood's fundamental instability. Because wood is exposed to weather, it undergoes repeated cycles of wetting and drying. Meanwhile oil-base paint loses its flexibility over time, and as the wood cracks so does the paint, allowing moisture into the wood and speeding up deterioration. To keep up with the brittleness of oil-base paint, you get into a never-ending maintenance routine to restore the peeling paint.

Unlike oil-base finishes acrylic-latex paints remain flexible enough to "breathe" with the wood as it moves. The paint tolerates exterior conditions better, but it's still not an ideal solution. As a film finish or top coat, it can still detach and peel from the surface.

Color stains are an even more practical solution and are highly recommended. The stain penetrates the wood and also seals it, giving with the wood as it weathers. Also stain is easier to maintain than paint. Instead of having to scrape it extensively as you would paint, in most cases you can merely sand the wood and then apply another coat or two of stain.

Unless you need a high-gloss sheen or a pure architectural white color, a solid-color stain is a user-friendly solution—easy to apply and easy to maintain.

Blue is the hue that lets this simple wall trellis take on a charming supportive role. Note how the color intensity is paired closely with the muted tones of the rose petals and the exposed brick in the wall. Careful color choice is essential. An intense version of this blue would be garish and overpowering, ruining the more poetic effect shown here.

TYPE OF FINISH	PROS	CONS
Oil-Base Enamel	Wide range of colors; sheen options include high gloss. Excellent color intensity. Creates a hard finish. Good durability on metal.	Becomes brittle with prolonged exposure to the elements; cracks form and allow moisture penetration in wood and accelerated paint failure. Deeper colors are prone to fading. Emits fumes of volatile organic compounds (VOC); cleanup requires solvents/paint thinners/mineral spirits.
Acrylic/Latex Enamel	Wide range of colors and sheen options, but not as high gloss as oil-base. Retains flexibility for compatibility with wood movement. No hazardous fumes; water cleanup.	Mechanical bond to surface can eventually fail, producing peeling. Not as hard as oil-base enamel.
Solid-Color Stain	Penetrates wood surface and even masonry to provide better bond. No hazardous fumes; most are latex or water-cleanup formulas. Minimal surface prep to renew or recoat.	Produces only a matte or low-sheen finish. Color choices not as extensive as for paints; difficult to get pure white. Not suitable for nonporous surfaces.

Garden Structure Kits

Kits are a trade-off between ready-made convenience and custom design, between paying just for materials and paying for labor. For this reason kits are increasingly available and popular, and the majority of some garden structures, such as gazebos, are now built from kits.

The quality of materials in kits tends to be good or excellent, though joinery techniques tend toward the basic to allow for mass production and so that beginners can manage the assembly. You can choose from a catalog of stock designs, and while you may find many you like, most won't look custom tailored to your site. (Some manufacturers provide custom versions but at higher prices.) On the plus side every part is precut and all the hardware is packaged and ready to use, so it's a great option for those with little building experience. Most kits are made of wood, but if white's your color and you want a no-maintenance result, consider buying vinyl.

From simple ready-to-assemble trellises under $50 to fancy gazebos topping $10,000, kits are found at home and garden centers, from specialty catalog retailers, and direct from manufacturers that sell their products online.

However even with a kit, site preparation is still your responsibility. (See page 24.) Figure that into the total cost of the project.

(See page 24.)

WHAT TO LOOK FOR IN A KIT

- Specific quality grades of materials (kiln-dried clear cedar or redwood)
- Complete set of required hardware and fasteners
- Affordable shipping costs
- Comprehensive instructions with good illustrations and photos; some even have videos
- Toll-free phone access to technical help 24/7
- Factory-finish options (often superior to site-applied finishes because they can be applied in controlled conditions with highly specialized equipment)

The various angles on this gazebo frame and roof would make it tough for all but the most accomplished amateur to design and build from scratch. A kit removes that hurdle, allowing you to assemble the components by following relatively simple directions. Concrete pier footings (see page 25) are still required for support, but most kit manufacturers provide diagrams to make that part of the job easier.

In kit form, small structures such as this arbor usually ship for a reasonable cost and can be finished in just a weekend. A prefabricated curved arch is a real timesaver, and trellis panels add more interest. Most projects call for site-built masonry footings.

Construction Primer

Given the variety of outdoor structures to choose from, it follows that construction methods will run the gamut as well. Installing a small freestanding trellis could mean little more than pressing the base into the soil. Building an elaborate pavilion might start with a bulldozer in your backyard and end with a crew of experienced finish carpenters wielding state-of-the-art tools.

Every project has its own sequence and complexity, but as a rule garden structures follow a general sequence of construction:

1: SITE PREPARATION

This might mean digging deep holes for concrete pier footings, excavating soil from a slope, or grading the surface for a brick paver patio. Before the first shovel hits dirt, however, call your local utility locating service and ask to have any underground pipes or electrical lines marked; the service is usually free and is usually required by law whenever you dig.

Most anything with a footprint smaller than 100 square feet can be managed by one or two people using manual tools. For bigger projects or where difficult conditions exist, prep work might require a skid-steer loader, a concrete mixer, or other large equipment. Unless you have experience and a good rental yard nearby, most of this heavy work is best left to professionals. It's dirty work and often tedious, but getting it right is vital to later phases of the project. Your participation should come in the form of detailed discussions with your contractor to ensure the techniques and results you want, especially for critical foundation work that won't be visible later.

2: CONCRETE AND MASONRY WORK

Footings, bases, and other concrete and masonry work take time. After it's constructed it may require up to a week for proper curing. Meanwhile other materials can be brought onsite, organized, cut as necessary, and even finished. Expect some chaos and noise; generators, air compressors, and other power tools may be in regular use.

3: OVERALL ASSEMBLY

Assembly typically begins with setting posts, beams, and other large structural parts. Good builders make frequent quality checks during this process, ensuring that the structure is level, square, and securely anchored. Care taken early allows the subsequent detail work to go quickly and consistently, so don't be impressed by a builder who hurries through the early parts of the job.

4: FINISH WORK

This stage can seem painstakingly slow and unproductive, depending on the project type and complexity. Typically trim work, painting, hardware installation, and other "small" tasks are completed at this time. Such work is often time consuming and—if there's a lot of it to do—accounts for a significant percentage of the overall project cost. By virtue of their relative simplicity, garden structures tend to require less of this detail work than interior projects do.

5: LANDSCAPING

Landscaping represents the final project stage in terms of execution, but it should be in your plans from the beginning. Plantings will soften the surroundings of a garden structure and, when mature, help create a more natural setting. If you are experienced with plants and know what you want in your garden, landscaping is an ideal do-it-yourself undertaking. If not don't expect your building contractor to handle this part of the project; a specialist such as a landscape designer or horticulturist will be better prepared to recommend and install plants.

TOOLS OF THE TRADE

The right tools can be the difference between a job that gets done quickly and well and a job that doesn't. When building an outdoor structure, consider the following:

Big ticket items that usually are most economical when rented:
- Power posthole auger
- Sod cutter
- Concrete mixer

Highly useful power tools:
- Power circular saw or miter saw
- 12-volt or larger cordless drill (with assorted drill and driver bits)
- Portable jigsaw

Basic woodworking tools:
- Framing hammer
- Builder's level
- 25-foot tape measure
- Wood chisel set
- String line
- Angle square

JOINING TIMBERS

Different types of joinery vary in their complexity and strength and cost when executed by a professional. Here are four common types of joinery.

Butted and Nailed
This simplest type of joinery is also the weakest.
1. Post
2. Galvanized nails
3. Beam

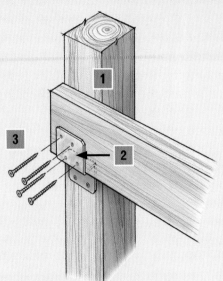

Framing Hardware with Screws
Using framing hardware on a butt joint adds strength quickly and fairly inexpensively.
1. Post
2. Galvanized metal framing bracket
3. Galvanized deck or sheet metal screws

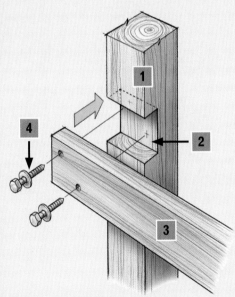

Notched and Bolted
The joint is superior and allows a heavier vertical load.
1. Post
2. Post notched to accept beam
3. Beam
4. Lag screws or hex bolts with washers

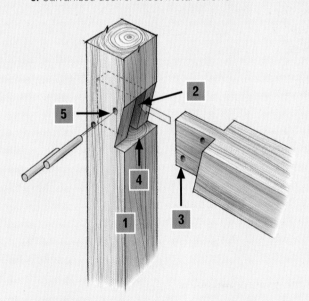

Pegged Mortise-and-Tenon
Complex and rather time consuming to make, this joint is noted for excellent strength and good looks (since no metal is involved).
1. Post
2. Mortise
3. Tenon
4. Haunch on which the beam rests
5. Drilled holes with wood pegs for security once tenon is fitted into mortise

Code Issues

The design and construction of any larger outdoor structure will likely be subject to building codes. City or county officials must approve the plans and issue a building permit, inspect the prepared site just before any concrete footings are poured, and make at least one more inspection to sign off on framing work or the completed structure.

Building codes govern such issues as a structure's proximity to property lines, its maximum footprint and height, framing techniques, structural soundness, and the use of appropriate materials. Most cities and towns use a standard international code book but also add their own interpretations or requirements. Separate codes apply specifically to electrical and plumbing work.

In many cases, a single permit will cover the entire project but multiple inspections usually are required to approve phases. (The permit usually states when an inspection is required before work can proceed further.)

Normally code requirements apply only to buildings of a certain type or size, especially if they don't involve any utility connections. In many towns most outdoor structures with a footprint smaller than 100 square feet may be built without a permit, so if your project is a simple trellis or arbor, odds are you won't need any kind of official inspections or design approval.

Whenever planning to do any digging, however minor, arrange for your local utility company to mark underground pipes and lines to prevent hitting them while you work.

The more complex and permanent an outdoor structure, the more likely it is to be subject to a variety of building codes that can dictate everything from positioning to height to building materials—and even overall design.

CONSTRUCTION CODE BASICS

Every legal jurisdiction handles code issues differently, but here are some common guidelines and rules you should expect to encounter.

- Never assume anything about which types of structures you can build on your property or whether you need a building permit. City or county officials will let you know the requirements.
- With all but the smallest structures, expect to pay a permit fee.
- Resist the temptation to "bootleg" your project (build illegally without the required permits). Any legitimate licensed contractor will obtain the necessary permits for the job. If you ignore this requirement, you may be forced to undo work (including removing the entire project) or pay fees and penalties, even years later when you're transferring the home to a new owner.

- You and/or your contractor must ensure that the project complies with code requirements. Even if city or county officials approve the plans and then note a violation upon inspection, they can deny a permit without bearing any legal responsibility for correcting the problem.
- Building codes don't specify every detail or anticipate every design option; they simply provide a minimum acceptable standard. Custom-built structures often exceed these minimums by featuring design and construction quality that's much higher than the law requires.
- Planned communities and designated historic districts often have private governing boards that regulate even small changes to residents' properties. Even if your city or county approves your plans or says no permit is needed, you could have other compliance issues.

Working With Contractors

Some homeowners are avid do-it-yourselfers who will easily tackle the design and construction of a garden structure and enjoy every minute of it. But if you'd rather hire the expertise and muscle, you'll still need to master one skill—working with contractors.

Finding and working with a contractor involves more than being able to communicate what you want. It also means evaluating and choosing the right builder, entering into a binding legal contract that protects both parties, and sorting out issues such as payment schedules and house rules before any work gets underway.

The project type, scale, and complexity will help you determine which contractors are appropriate. As with many trades, building involves subspecialties, and not every licensed contractor is qualified to perform the particular jobs you want done. If the project involves mostly carpentry work, a framing contractor or even a handyman service might do. Landscaping contractors often have their own building crews to handle such projects, as do small design/build firms.

For larger structures consider hiring a general contractor, who will manage the entire project and either provide a work crew or hire subcontractors to complete various parts of the job. Despite the mixed reputation of the building industry, most contractors are legitimate businesspeople intent on serving their clients professionally.

CONTRACTOR CHECKLIST

Here's how to find a good contractor and to make sure that your relationship ends happily.

❑ Be clear about what you want in your new structure. If you aren't sure, hire a landscape architect or residential designer to come up with a plan before you recruit a builder. Some builders may offer to design the structure for you or work from your sketches, but remember that you get what you pay for. Most contractors are skilled in building techniques and are not necessarily adept at scale, form, balance, and other aesthetics.

❑ Do a routine background check with your state contractors license board or local Better Business Bureau on current license, insurance coverage, and any formal complaints registered against a contractor. This advice is a cliché for a reason—simple precautions can weed out contractors with a poor track record.

❑ Get multiple bids. Everyone hears this advice, but not all heed it. You cannot make an informed decision about price, design, or quality without having the context that comes from talking to several contractors. Be willing to pay for bid proposals if the project is large.

❑ See their work. Even if friends or neighbors have offered a glowing referral, make it a point to see prior work firsthand. Everyone's standards and ideas about quality are a little different.

❑ If your gut impression is poor, move on. Never hire a contractor who shows up significantly late or not at all for your initial appointment, thinks he or she knows what you want better than you do, doesn't return phone calls within 24 hours, or exhibits other unprofessional habits; these bad behaviors only get worse. The worst-case scenario is that the person takes on the project and then abandons it in the middle, leaving you with a half-finished structure and perhaps not enough of your budget remaining to hire someone new.

❑ Get specifics in writing. A good contract spells out start and finish dates, materials quality, procedures for change orders, payment schedule, consequences of default, crew and subcontractor management, and any other significant legal or jobsite issues. Especially nice (although rare) is contract language specifying that the contractor will take a cut in pay if the project runs late due to circumstances within his or her control.

❑ Establish the house rules. Where can company trucks and crew vehicles park? Can workers use a bathroom, and if so which one? Is smoking allowed onsite? Is there access to an electrical outlet from the house? Which trees, plants, and other landscape features need to be protected? Make sure everyone has answers to these questions.

❑ Share the financial risks. Up-front payments for a job should typically run between 10 and 30 percent of the total cost, with interim payments agreed upon and tied to job progress. At least 10 percent should be withheld until all work is complete and inspected. Avoid any contractor who wants the entire payment up front.

❑ Expect to be promotional material. A contractor may refer potential clients to see your project later, a reasonable courtesy to extend if you are happy with the outcome.

Budgeting Time and Money

Having several contractors bid on your garden structure will give you a pretty good idea of how much money and time are required to build it. But because so many variables are involved, it's often impossible to pinpoint exact project costs ahead of time. The scale, complexity, and quality of materials are the three biggest factors in determining the cost of a project, but the local economy and labor market count also.

Typically you can expect materials to account for only one-fourth to one-third of a project's overall budget. The rest goes to labor, overhead, and profit margins for the contractor. If you have the skills, tools, and willingness to get the project done by rolling up your own sleeves, your project dollars will go that much farther. In that case it's especially worthwhile to divert some of the cost savings to pay for professional design help.

Project costs are determined by many things. The beautiful bell-shape roof and corbel trim on this gazebo obviously make it more expensive. But costs can be jacked up by other factors, such as the secluded setting, which provides delightful privacy but also restricts construction vehicle access and requires some materials to be carried by hand.

BASIC CONTRACT TYPES

Fixed Bid Contracts
These are just what the name suggests, a prearranged package price that includes all the work and materials spelled out in the contract. It offers the advantage of a known quantity, but most contractors allow for surprise cost overruns and build them into the bid. You pay this premium even if the job runs like a Swiss watch.

Cost Plus Contracts.
These contracts reduce the mystery some by having the contractor bill you for specific labor and materials charges and then adding a certain percentage for overhead and profit. You know more details about specific itemized costs, but there's not much incentive for contractors to be efficient because they get their cut regardless.

Time and Materials Contracts.
These allow flexibility for projects that may hold some surprises. A specified hourly labor rate is charged and materials costs are billed directly, sometimes with a small markup. Open-ended agreements can let costs climb to unacceptable levels; protect yourself with a "not to exceed" spending cap or one that offers a labor discount for amounts above the cost estimate.

TYPICAL COSTS FOR GARDEN STRUCTURES*

Though each garden structure is different, you can estimate the range you might spend according to the type of structure.

Freestanding Trellis
Do-it-yourself: $75–$500
Kit: $150–$1,000
Contractor-built: $250 for simple versions; up to $1,500

Arbor
Do-it-yourself: $150–$750
Kit: $250–$1,000
Contractor-built: $400 for simple versions; up to $2,500

Pergola
Do-it-yourself: $500–$1,500
Kit: $1,000–$2,500
Contractor-built: $1,500 for simple versions; up to $5,000

Gazebo
Do-it-yourself: $1,000–$2,500
Kit: $1,500–$5,000
Contractor-built: $2,500 for simple versions; up to $10,000

*Estimated; costs can vary widely

2 Trellises

The most basic of garden structures, trellises are relatively simple and inexpensive to build, supportive of your plants, and protective of your privacy. Few other features in your yard are so affordable or versatile: They allow you to effectively shape the landscape, creating focal points and—where desired—limiting views.

Trellises are team players, perfectly happy with a supporting role. In addition to offering a home to climbing plants, they make invaluable accessories for larger structures such as arbors, fences, and pergolas.

🌼 About Trellises

For something so small, a trellis can do so much.

Along with being just plain nice to look at, trellises allow you to create various visual effects in your garden. You can use trellises to add height, either for balance or to compensate for a lack of tall trees or other vertical elements in the landscape.

You can also use trellises to fully or partially block unpleasant views. This makes them especially useful around the perimeter of a yard or to create defining borders between garden areas. They're also excellent near sitting areas where privacy is desired.

Trellises can also be used to break up wide expanses of solid wall or to camouflage unattractive or deteriorating building materials, such as concrete block, chain link fences, splintering wood, or problem siding.

Since trellises tend to be simple, inexpensive structures, use them creatively and lavishly. Experiment with various materials and make the trellises as small or as large as your heart desires.

A small trellis, just the right size for a diminutive vine, say, no more than 6 feet, can be made from a few pieces of lumber or several branches.

Very large trellises are really elaborate fences or walls that can stretch dozens of feet long and rise 6 or even 8 feet high. They can cover an entire fence or the entire side of a building.

Whatever the size of the trellis, the key to success is regular spacing. Although trellises were originally designed to support climbing plants in those spaces, the structure can be left bare to provide shelter and shade if the trelliswork is especially nice.

The open weave of a trellis can serve as a frame that draws attention to various details in a garden. Here the outline of the trellis and the sunlight dramatically accentuate the beauty of a climbing rose in bloom.

This whimsical twig structure illustrates how simple trellises can be, and how much character they can add to a garden. With nothing more than a handful of natural branches and a few nails to secure them, a trellis like this costs just pennies and can be put together in an hour or two. The rounded twigs create an intriguing interplay between light and shadow.

Simple Wall-Mounted Trellises

Wall-mounted trellises take up zero ground space and can be a major feature in a garden. They're easy to install and don't become wobbly the way some freestanding trellises can. Best of all, they can transform a wall or side of a garage or other building from blah to beautiful. Especially when custom made to cover the side of a garage, they add elegance to a basic (and sometimes problematic) structure.

Because a wall-mounted trellis is literally connected to the house or another building on the site, it usually pays to create a clear stylistic tie as well. You can achieve your goal by including some design details borrowed from the building. The trellis will look more like an architectural feature than a garden accessory, making the effect seem more deliberate and less of an afterthought. Cottage- or rustic-style homes are more forgiving of informal mismatches than pure period-style homes are, but as a general rule try to respect the look of the house.

Take a cue from the material used in the siding (wood on wood is always good). Use a trim color for contrast or go with the same color as the siding. Introducing an entirely new color seldom works, but if you want the trellis to stand out as an independent architectural detail, go ahead and paint it a lively shade.

These especially attractive, well-designed lattice panels support vines and are accented with faux columns that echo the actual functioning column in the background. They turn what could be a nothing space between two buildings into an elegant courtyard.

HOW TO MOUNT A TRELLIS

Most trellises are fairly simple to install. Follow these tips to make sure yours is mounted wisely.

- Whenever possible choose a wall that has some roof overhang to offer the trellis protection from direct rainfall and ensure a longer life.
- Make sure the trellis grid size and other details are compatible with any plants you want to train on it. Trumpet vine and other rampant growers may be fine on a very large grid, but plants that prefer a denser mesh, such as sweet pea, may struggle.
- Don't start drilling until you test fit the trellis; step back to get a better idea of which placement looks best.
- Don't go overboard putting holes in the wall, but be sure to secure small trellises at a minimum of two points, more for larger sizes. Wind gusts can lift or tear off a trellis that isn't adequately fastened.
- Use small blocks or spacers at mounting points to keep the trellis from direct contact with the wall surface. The gap allows for drainage and helps deter aggressive climbing plants from penetrating the siding.
- On wood or wood composite siding use corrosion-resistant screws and make sure they penetrate at least into the solid plywood sheathing if not the wall framing itself.
- On stucco, concrete, and other masonry surfaces use a carbide-tipped masonry drill to bore holes for expansion anchors. Thread the proper screws into the anchors to secure them. On brick walls, drill and install anchors in the mortar joints, not in the brick faces.

This simple trellis features a cedar frame and two inserts cut from a vinyl lattice panel. Installed to train a small ficus tree on a covered deck, it matches the surrounding trim and is meant to be seen.

The unfinished cedar shingle siding on this garage offers the perfect backdrop for a fanciful heart-shape trellis. Because both the siding and trellis are unfinished, it's important to use spacers to provide an air gap between the two structures.

Incorporating Circles

There's just something special about circles. Maybe it's because outdoor structures are usually all straight lines and right angles because those are easier to make than circles, which take a higher level of construction skill. But when planned wisely circles are not difficult to form and they can turn an ordinary garden structure into something extraordinary.

Because circles take a little extra care, you seldom find them in premade garden accents and structures. That's why they're so striking when included in a custom structure, where they add an element of quality.

There are many different ways to incorporate circles into garden structures. On these pages circular insets have been built into a trellis design. (Also see page 111 for information on how to create a circular opening in a latticework panel.)

When considering incorporating circles for a structure or design, look around to see if there are other circles in the landscape or in nearby architecture that you could mimic, and thus give the landscape a subtle feeling of unity. Look to windows, pavement, garden ornaments, or even the shapes of beds and borders for inspiration.

Although a structure with circles can look at home even if there aren't other circles in the landscape, if it can mimic the size or details of other circles, it will fit into the overall setting even better.

In landscapes where so many of the lines are straight, circles of any sort break the rigid geometry and add a satisfying element. These circles serve as surprising apertures in the latticework, drawing the eye to the trellis and the rose scaling it.

MAKING CIRCLES IN A TRELLIS

Construction and and fitting of these seemly complex circles is not difficult once you understand how they're constructed.

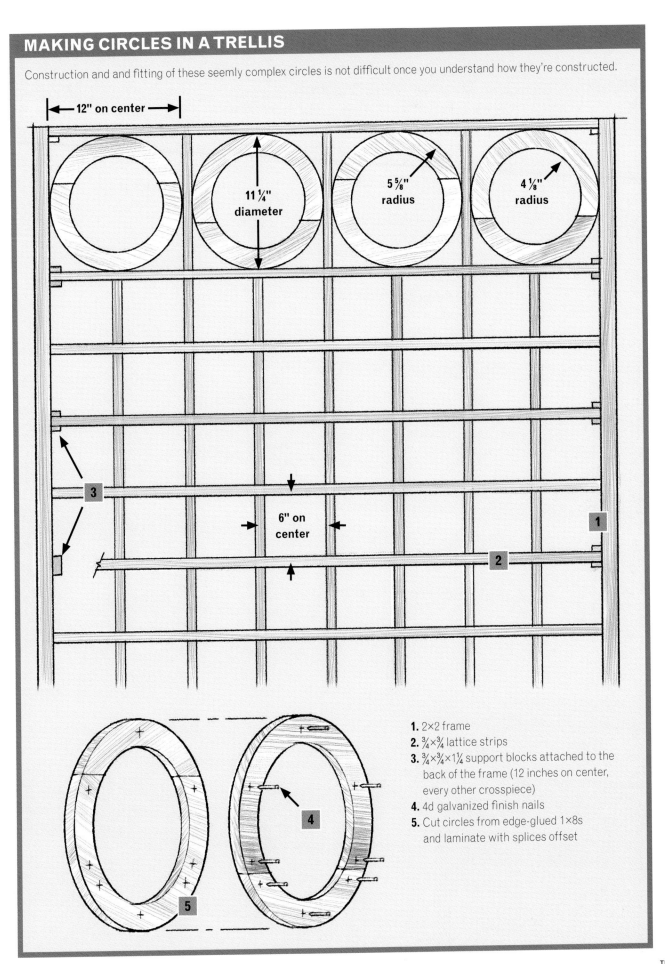

12" on center

11 ¼" diameter

5 ⅝" radius

4 ⅛" radius

6" on center

3

1

2

4

5

1. 2×2 frame
2. ¾×¾ lattice strips
3. ¾×¾×1¼ support blocks attached to the back of the frame (12 inches on center, every other crosspiece)
4. 4d galvanized finish nails
5. Cut circles from edge-glued 1×8s and laminate with splices offset

Incorporating Curved Tops

A simple curved top on a trellis can add big visual impact. As with circles and other curved designs in construction, it bespeaks a certain quality and attention to detail that's hard to find in most premade structures.

The construction basics are surprisingly easy enough that you can incorporate this appealing feature without creating a logistical or budgetary monster. (See page 120 for how-to tips and techniques on making arches and other curved components for garden structures.)

The little bit of extra time and attention is worthwhile. Because curved tops nudge your gaze upward, they tend to lighten a structure visually. And while the lower portion of a trellis often gets obscured by foliage from a climbing plant, a curved top rail usually stays visible, so the extra effort to include it doesn't go unrewarded. A curved top also makes it easy to introduce other accents, such as keystone trim or post finials.

Especially on larger, more massive structures, curved tops have a softening effect. A large trelliswork fence, for example, might become a vast expanse of gridwork—but with a curved top the structure gains a certain charm and softness that prevents it from feeling oppressive.

This is a landscape of curves. There are curves in the furniture, the stone balls, and also in the swooping lines of the latticework fence and arbor.

This side yard path offers an unexpected vista—a pair of graceful trellises topped with curved rails and flanked by stout posts and finials. The curved tops help alleviate the long, straight lines and make the trellises more significant and special, transforming a narrow nothing side yard into a pretty vignette.

These simple rectangular trellises show strength in numbers. Individually none is large or prominent enough to serve as an architectural feature. Mounted in a series, however, they take on a bigger presence that commands attention.

Designing Wall-Mounted Trellises

A wall-mounted trellis can be nothing short of a miracle worker. It can transform an imperfect side of a building into an architectural delight and turn a boring fence into a striking focal point or elegant backdrop for the rest of the garden. And it can break up large expanses of building walls, adding architectural interest that visually softening greenery can scramble up.

In planning a wall-mounted trellis, think big. Undersize trellises can look sadly skimpy or simply get lost in the landscape. While the scale doesn't have to be enormous, it needs to be large enough to have an impact. Tiny trellises get lost amid other features.

When designing and building the trellis, go for strength. Too many homeowners quickly put up something made from the cheapest materials available, but with any luck a well-made trellis will last for many years and perhaps even several decades.

Keep in mind how the trellis will interact with the surface on which it's mounted. Be sure to provide space behind a trellis mounted on wood to allow for some circulation to prevent moisture problems.

It's a myth that a trellis always will contribute to the decay of wood siding. In hot, dry climates, for example, it can actually shade and protect siding.

With its arched center panel and precisely fitted framework, this trellis effectively transforms the humble dog-eared wood fence that supports it. The classic pattern also suggests a doorway, giving the surface the enchanting illusion of depth.

Freestanding Trellises

Although often simple structures, trellises that stand on their own can perform important tasks, including adding vertical elements to new gardens, serving as almost sculptural focal points, screening views, and adding color and structure to a yard. They also, of course, are great for supporting favorite climbing plants.

Even small trellises need good footing in the ground (see page 25 for methods of anchoring them) or else wind, snow, or a large vine will topple them.

Certainly the small premade trellises that are just a few feet wide and maybe 6 feet tall are fine for simply inserting into the ground (though even they tend to go wobbly and do better when backed up with some stakes screwed into the back for extra support).

Anything larger needs substantial support. Footings of sand, gravel, and/or concrete are a must, especially since the trellis is most likely to lean or topple when you least want it to—in the middle of the summer when the vine trained on it has reached its pinnacle of fullness and the trellis is looking its glorious best.

This trellis was built as a way station along a garden walkway, but it would also be a beautiful focal point at the end of a narrow yard. It displays a subtle and engaging mix of elements. Shorter end panels—featuring small-weave trellises—flank a taller section with a more open grid trellis and an unexpected round window.

This classic three-section trellis adds structure and definition to the planting area. It also screens a work area in the garden.

TIPS FOR PLACING FREESTANDING TRELLISES

- **Don't just plunk them anywhere.** They need to have a relationship to the walls and fences around them. Place them along a wall, at a 45-degree angle, at the end of a path, or in some other way that makes sense.
- **Use smaller trellises in a group** to avoid their looking dinky. Consider using at least three small trellises placed in a line at equal distances for more impact. Or flank a door with matching trellises.
- **Break up large spaces.** So many trellises are a vast expanse of premade latticework, which looks oppressive and monotonous. Break up the expanse with a design element such as a different kind of grid or an aperture (see page 57).
- **Be bold with materials.** Consider working wire, mesh, steel bars, or other materials into your trellis. A mixture adds interest and distinctiveness.
- **Be bold with color.** A trellis left natural or painted white is classic, but consider the many other colors that can make the structure unique (see page 41).

The mixed gridwork on this bamboo trellis suggests a tall building emerging from an Asian-style rock garden, all portrayed on a diminutive scale. Crafted from bamboo it fits perfectly in this Asian-inspired garden and provides a much-needed backdrop to the plantings.

Freestanding Trellises

When most people think of trellises, they imagine simple small structures. But shown here are trellises that stretch beyond the traditional with useful as well as decorative variations on the trellis theme.

A trellis can be an extension of a fence—a lovely way to define an entrance, especially in a more casual setting, such as a back door or the area leading from a garage or driveway into the landscape.

With a little ingenuity a trellis can be designed to solve the problem of people cutting across corner flower gardens. The trellis can block foot traffic and also provide a visual anchor for the flowerbed. This type of trellis could just as easily create a pleasant nook when attached to a deck.

The larger the trellis the less it is an accent and the more it is a wall. Trellises can rise just a few feet high, like a low fence, or tower to 8 or more feet like the trellis on the opposite page. This trellis, surrounded by trees, serves as a focal point and a backdrop for lush plantings.

With none of the confining feel of a fence or solid wall, this trellis grouping clearly defines an entrance to a patio area beyond. You could step inside, settle in at an outdoor table, and dine in a relaxed manner, even though the literal separation from outside elements is very slight.

Large trellises can be used as walls in outdoor rooms. This trellis adds a distinctive back wall to this room. It also creates a cozy place to sit and view the sundial and lush plantings.

This simple trellis stands guard at the corner of a small raised bed. Use such a trellis to block foot traffic in a corner garden. Or go with four trellises to define the four corners of a garden.

Trellises as a Privacy Solution

A trellis can provide privacy in a way no solid fence or wall can. Inviting and airy, trellises are nowhere near as oppressive or confining as solid structures. They also take up minimal ground space, so you can get lots of privacy by committing just inches of precious yard, deck, or patio.

Where tall fencing isn't an appropriate or legal solution (most communities have height limits for fences), trellises can substitute and sometimes do an even better job. They aren't as harsh looking as solid fences or walls, and most allow you to retain some of your outbound views without really giving up any privacy.

On the other hand, have realistic expectations for your trellis. Some homeowners plant vines expecting that they'll immediately cover the trellis. But growing a thick curtain of foliage can take years and if the vine is deciduous, the screen is effective only during the summer months when the vine is fully leafed out.

Instead view a privacy trellis as something that provides more psychological privacy than visual privacy, something that delineates one space from another and sets it apart with a mere suggestion of a screen between.

Even though these trellises are easy to see through, they still screen views from the sitting area and help define a relaxed seating place in what could otherwise be an uncomfortably open area.

This stylish lath surround feels very midcentury modern, making it a perfect candidate for a house of that era. The built-in cushioned seating is practical and also provides a sense of privacy by blocking views.

DESIGNING TRELLISES FOR PRIVACY

- Limit trellis height to about eye level, or just under 6 feet; this allows privacy but doesn't feel like an oppressive enclosure.
- Integrate a privacy trellis with a deck railing, built-in seating, or some other feature that makes its function less conspicuous.
- Limit openings to a maximum of 3 inches unless you will have year-round plant coverage on the trellis.
- In all but the warmest regions vines add privacy during only part of the year. Design privacy trellises so that they're functional even when vines aren't cloaking them.

With its wraparound form and projecting top, this trellis ensemble offers privacy in a delightful and relaxing setting. The sense of shelter is unmistakable without a claustrophobic enclosed feeling. A pair of cushioned chairs is the only invitation necessary.

Trellises as a Privacy Solution

Trellises can have different roles when it comes to screening a view. The most obvious is to afford you some privacy from the street or from neighbors' yards. But sometimes you'll want to screen views within your own yard.

For example, air-conditioning units and garbage can storage areas are good candidates for trellises that mask the unsightly stuff and add a decorative effect. You might want to shield features such as a hot tub, or subdivide spaces within your yard such as an outdoor dining area to set apart from the rest of the landscape. As with most garden structures, you need only create the suggestion of the effect, what designers call a gesture. If you succeed in your gesture, then actually blocking the view is unnecessary as well as undesirable.

In fact closing off the view with a solid surface means blocking your own outward view, which tends to trigger anxiety or restlessness instead of a sense of security. For example, a sitting space surrounded by a 6-foot trellis is more inviting than one enclosed by a 6-foot-tall solid fence. The fence would make the area feel more like a prison than a retreat. A solid structure also blocks breezes, so you might as well be inside.

Keep in mind that you can vary the height of a trellis. You might want it 6 feet in one portion to provide privacy and only 4 feet elsewhere to create a sense of enclosure or to hold a low growing but sprawling vine.

Outdoor areas take on instant charm when a sense of privacy is established. This latticework trellis provides an appealing backdrop for a cafe table and chairs. Without the screening the setting would seem too exposed and far less inviting.

Building a Bamboo Trellis

Sawn lumber might be the most common material used for building trellises, but it's certainly not the only option. Especially in warmer regions of the country, bamboo is just one of several alternative materials that are increasingly popular in gardens.

And bamboo is almost as simple to work with as wood. Bamboo technically is a grass, but it's actually harder than many woods. It can be machined and processed to make finished products such as flooring, but bamboo for garden structures is typically used in a more natural form—as a round cane or split into slats.

Many varieties are imported into the United States, in diameters commonly ranging from about ½ inch to 5 inches. Sizes larger than 2 inches in diameter are often referred to as bamboo lumber because they are used as structural posts and beams.

Bamboo structures are ideal for creating an Asian flavor in a garden, but the material is not perfect. Like most woods it degrades from exposure to harsh weather conditions and it becomes increasingly brittle with age. It's relatively easy to work with and to replace and it contributes to a more natural look in a garden.

These bamboo trellis panels add a great visual texture to a wood fence and offer a useful scaffold for climbing plants. The panels feature a woven construction and use bamboo slats rather than full round cane.

CONSTRUCTING A BAMBOO TRELLIS

Making a bamboo trellis is much easier if you know a few tricks for working with this lightweight but tough material.

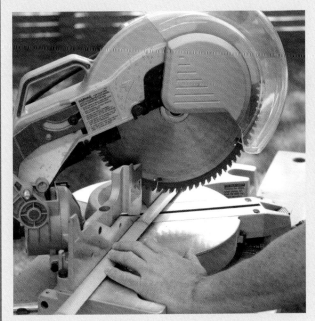

Step 1: If possible order bamboo strips or staves rather than round cane. (Otherwise you have to rip the cane into strips on a table saw or pay a local woodworking shop to do it for you.) Decide on the trellis panel size and lay out strips to form the outer frame, then cut the diagonal strips to length with a power miter saw.

Step 2: Bamboo is tough but brittle when dry, so always drill holes for fasteners or tied connections. Here a $\frac{1}{8}$-inch drill bit is used to make holes for the tie wires. Where possible weave the bamboo slats and drill them in place so the holes align correctly.

Step 3: A 16-gauge galvanized utility wire works great for threading through the holes and tying the slats together. Start at one corner and work your way across; the job gets easier as you progress.

Tuteurs and Obelisks

Derived from the French word for tutor or guardian, freestanding multisided supports called tuteurs (too-TOURS) support plants as they grow upward. They're a classic especially in rose gardens where they are used to train roses with long, arching canes upward, turning them into pillar or climbing roses.

The most basic tuteurs are merely posts with cross-arms or string lines attached. But the most popular types resemble tapered cages or tepee frameworks. Rustic versions often feature willow branches wrapped in a conical shape, but there are many variations on this simple theme.

Obelisks are a specific type of tuteur, featuring flat sides and an elongated pyramidal shape. Their geometry—specifically the sharp angles at the top—can make them a little harder to construct. For this reason, many premade or partly assembled tuteurs and obelisks are available in a variety of materials, especially wood and metal.

Tuteurs and obelisks can rise a couple of feet or they can tower to 8 feet or more. Most are 4 to 6 feet tall, which is the height of most shorter climbing vines (see page 214 for listings of recommended vines for garden structures).

Tuteurs and obelisks supports can be used solo but are great in groups. Use two to flank the beginning of a path or at the entrance to a house (they're attractive in pots). Use one in each corner of a square or rectangular bed. Or arrange three, five, or more in a straight line running through a large flowerbed.

IDEAS FOR USING TUTEURS AND OBELISKS

Tuteurs and obelisks traditionally are plant supports, but the fact is that they're so attractive they can be used in a variety of ways, including without plants (but in a bed) as a sort of functional sculpture. Here are some ideas for placing the structures.

- Use them in groups. Try placing three, five, or more (odd numbers look most attractive from a design perspective) in a line throughout a large bed.
- Place one in each corner of a vegetable garden for pole beans, peas, and other climbers to scramble up.
- Push smaller ones into large pots and planters.
- Position one on either side of a front or back door (in pots or not) or on either side of a path or entry into a garden.
- Use several in a line on either side of a path for an abbreviated version of a classic French allée.

Tuteurs offer a set-it-and-forget-it ease to gardening, especially when combined with containers. This simple curved version serves as a graceful ornament in addition to providing support for the plants, and the beaded finial echoes the shape of the terra-cotta pot below.

Even though it's actively supporting only a handful of the plants in the flowerbed, this obelisk lends structure to the garden area simply through its strong geometry and form. The yellow-green wood blends with the garden but also provides a playful touch.

This copper trellis features all three basic types of the material: rigid copper pipe and fittings for the framework, flexible copper tubing for the arched top rail, and solid copper wire for the accents. A single trip to the hardware store or home center provides all the tools and materials needed for this one-of-a-kind project.

Building With Copper

Tuteurs and small trellises are ideal projects for experimenting with copper as a building material. Copper is easy to work with and doesn't require a lot of specialized or expensive tools, although it is relatively expensive and is better suited to small-scale structures.

Unless you intend to seek out an industrial metal supplier for top-dollar specialty copper, choices for copper are limited to three basic materials: flexible tubing (sold by the foot from large coils), rigid copper pipe (sold in straight 10-foot lengths, with fittings to connect joints and turn corners), and solid bare copper wire (sold by the foot or spool). Even these materials are pricey, especially in the larger tubing and pipe sizes (up to 1-inch at most home centers), so keep project designs modest in scale.

Don't mix copper with other metals except brass (a copper alloy). Contact with dissimilar metals such as steel causes a harsh corrosive reaction that will discolor and weaken both metals.

However copper's tendency to interact with its environment is what can make it so wonderful outdoors, especially in a garden. As it develops a patina over the months, it blends into the natural setting, making it look as though it's always been there and giving the landscape a restful, established look.

The top of this tuteur is actually easier to build in copper than in wood. The elbow fittings—45 degrees at each leg and a pair of 90-degree elbows at the peak—ensure easy alignment as long as you cut the straight pipe sections to consistent lengths. There's no fitting available to join all four top rails at the angle shown, so the peak is made from two sections, one tucked just below the other.

THE BASICS OF WORKING WITH COPPER

Copper adds instant class to a garden. It starts out shiny when it's new but quickly ages to a patina that is closer to bronze, then darkens, and finally develops that wonderful gray-brown-green surface.

Building with copper means using something other than standard carpentry tools. In fact most of the tools you'll be using can be found in the plumbing and electrical section of a home improvement store. You can cut copper tubing and pipe with a tubing cutter, which features a small cutting disk and an adjustable clamping roller. The disk scores the surface as you rotate the cutter around the pipe, tightening until the pipe is severed.

As the name suggests, flexible copper tubing can be bent into curved shapes, but trying to force sharp angles only causes it to kink or collapse. Use flexible tubing for arches and other gradual bends. You can shape the curve freehand or, if more precision is required, make a wood bending form with a curved edge.

Rigid copper pipe in ½- or ¾-inch sizes is good for making structures with straight lines and regular angles. Fittings such as elbows (with 90-, 45-, or 22½-degree angles) and tees let you form corners and connect short lengths of pipe into larger assemblies. When used for plumbing these slip fittings are soldered on with a propane torch, but you can use a metal epoxy or similar adhesive to put a trellis together since it won't have to be watertight.

Solid copper wire is best suited for twisting into accent pieces or for tying parts together. (Don't use stranded wire because it won't hold its shape as well when bent.) Common sizes are 14 through 6 gauge, with the lower numbers indicating larger diameters. A lineman's pliers features a side-cutting jaw and also textured flat jaws for gripping and twisting; for tight bends or fine work you can use needle-nose pliers.

Using Found or Repurposed Materials

Simplicity is an underrated virtue of trellises, one that lets you take liberties with eclectic materials and whimsical designs. There's not really any complex engineering for carrying heavy loads or spanning large distances, so you can pick materials based on their looks and personality instead of their muscle power.

Using found or repurposed objects as sculpture or ornament is a well-established tradition in garden design. These objects become instant focal points, and many of them have features that encourage plants to make themselves at home. The next time you're at a flea market or salvage store and spot an old window sash or a vintage wrought-iron headboard, think trellis potential.

Combine new and old materials. Perhaps join two old wooden columns into one trellis with the addition of steel bars or new latticework. Or as shown below, turn an open window frame into a trellis with the addition of chicken wire and sturdy posts to support it. (Also try experimenting with steel and copper wire, woven or strung, or other types of wire mesh, combined with vintage pieces.)

Or combine two old pieces, as with the door frame remnant and rusty fencing shown on the opposite page. Play around with combinations, such as old screen doors hinged together to make a screen.

And while many of the old finishes on these pieces is part of their charm, especially when combining very different elements, consider a coat of fresh paint, either white or a playful color such as purple, spring green, or pale blue.

Suspended from a rustic frame consisting of tree branches, this former window assembly keeps its ornate classical trim but trades glass panes for chicken wire.

(Top left) With found objects it's all about attitude. This scrappy iron headboard was probably tossed out due to its aged condition, but it creates instant charm as a wall-mounted trellis.

(Top right) Once-ordinary items like this rusted wire fencing lend a nostalgic air to garden decor when repurposed as a trellis for a clematis. The painted wood casing and rosette block will weather over time, contributing even more to the vintage character.

(Bottom) An old window frame, complete with an arched transom, was fitted with a cedar grid and now serves to support a large vine. There's more interest here than either trellis or plant alone could offer.

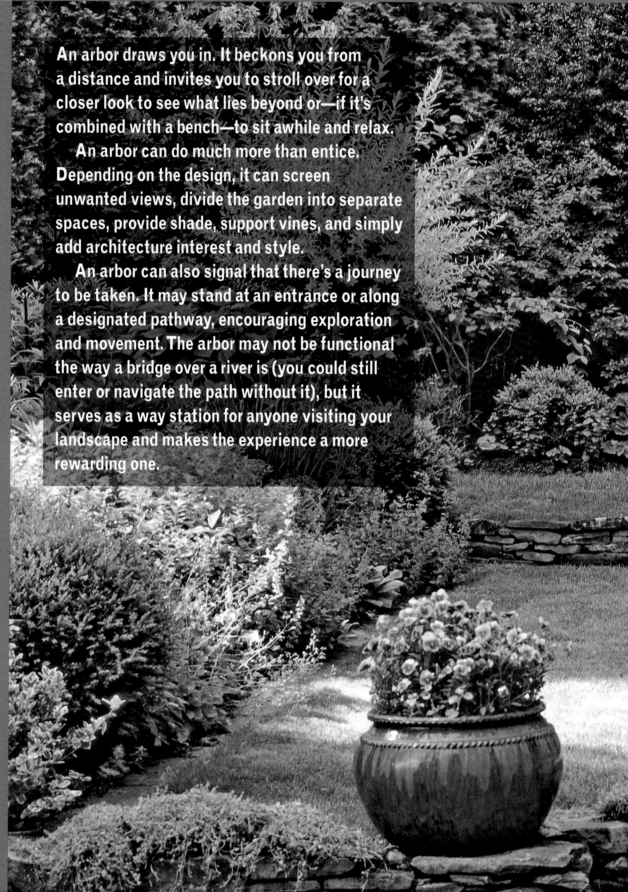

3 Arbors

An arbor draws you in. It beckons you from a distance and invites you to stroll over for a closer look to see what lies beyond or—if it's combined with a bench—to sit awhile and relax.

An arbor can do much more than entice. Depending on the design, it can screen unwanted views, divide the garden into separate spaces, provide shade, support vines, and simply add architecture interest and style.

An arbor can also signal that there's a journey to be taken. It may stand at an entrance or along a designated pathway, encouraging exploration and movement. The arbor may not be functional the way a bridge over a river is (you could still enter or navigate the path without it), but it serves as a way station for anyone visiting your landscape and makes the experience a more rewarding one.

About Arbors

As with so many garden structures, the definition of an arbor is a slightly blurry one. The doorway arbor, usually positioned at the start or finish of a garden path, is a familiar type. But there are other kinds as well, including the old-fashioned grape arbor. Some look very much like what you could call a pergola.

When reduced to its basic elements, an arbor consists simply of a pair of posts or a series of paired posts, topped by a crossbeam or other assembly that bridges the space between them. In scale an arbor can be as narrow as a standard doorway or as long as a small house. Most versions of an arbor feature some variation on the basic theme, such as added trellises that flank the posts, arched tops that create a more graceful line than a plain horizontal beam would, or a gate that swings between the posts.

The word "arbor" in Latin means tree and indeed an arbor typically mimics a tree's structure by pairing trunklike upright posts with a denser or more ornate top portion intended to provide shade. Often a vine or other plant is trained to grow onto the top, but even without foliage most arbors do offer some shelter from sunlight.

A SUCCESSFUL ARBOR IS...

- ... clearly positioned along a pathway or open space, encouraging exploration.
- ... built to an appropriate scale for the yard and home.
- ... connected to the landscape, either through surrounding plantings or attachment to trellises, fences, or other structures.
- ... securely anchored to the ground so wind or other stresses don't topple it (see page 25).
- ...one that makes you want to walk to it or through it, whether it be a simple two-post version or a continuing shaded "tunnel."

An arbor gives structure to a landscape. The best versions are focal points that beckon your gaze in and through, suggesting there's more to be found along the path.

This quiet courtyard setting shows off one of the great strengths of arbors as "announcements," that is, that you are about to enter an inviting place. Walking underneath these simple arches is a literal rite of passage here. A matching arbor on the other end echoes the formal design, reinforced by geometric planters and tightly clipped shrubs.

Although this beautiful Asian-influenced arbor looks complex, it's more about assembling simple components into a dramatic design and showcasing the tone of the wood than it is about ornate details or complex joinery. The focus on simple elements that don't attempt to hide the skills of the builder is also a hallmark of Arts and Crafts design, making this arbor a natural choice since it's in the landscape of a home of that period.

About Arbors

One of the wonderful characteristics of arbors is that they suggest and encourage movement, acting as a transition, like a doorway or a tunnel, from one garden area to another. And sometimes they're simply a delightful stopping point along a clearly marked path.

When you add a gate to an arbor, walking through it becomes almost irresistible. This psychological pull encourages visitors to tour your garden and adds a sense of journey to the space.

Some arbors include a bench or swing, and as with a gate, the extra element entices people to walk over to the structure and enjoy it. Because arbors have such strong beckoning power, you can use them to make small areas seem larger. It works this way: The farther away your gaze is directed, the greater the perception of space in front of you, making your yard seem larger and more interesting.

Although this adobe archway is part of a wall, the gateway role it plays for the patio area is all arbor. The hybrid design—part wall, part arbor—provides a good example of how garden structures can be closely tied to the architecture of the house and still work to define the outdoor environment.

❦ About Arbors

As you imagine an arbor in your landscape, think about how it will work with the rest of the space.

Too many arbors are just dropped into the middle of a yard, like a doorway or a hallway in the middle of nowhere, looking a little like a misplaced tollbooth. Arbors work best when placed along or next to other elements—either plants or other hardscape such as fences and paths.

Without such connections arbors look exposed and lonely. When positioned well arbors are highly evocative, suggesting that walking through or toward them is a relaxed and enjoyable journey in a landscape that's just the tiniest bit magical.

This wonderful purple-blue arbor is an excellent lesson on how a garden structure can change the feeling of a relatively small area. The whimsical color adds punch to the landscape and also contrasts well with the plantings.

With its strong geometry and well-defined role as a gated sentry, this arbor and its flanking trellises create a deliberately formal look, complemented by topiary shrubs in pots, a paved walkway, and an ivy-covered retaining wall.

Building a Classic Arbor

Like most other landscape elements, arbors come in various shapes, sizes, and colors, but they still have recognizable characteristics that define them.

The most obvious is an arch or beam that bridges two sides—the simplest arbors are essentially doorways. But arbors can be larger and more elaborate too. They can have a series of posts that create a structure something like a tunnel. A classic example is the grape arbors favored at the turn of the last century.

The arbor shown below could easily be dubbed a classic for its crisp white finish and the many details that make you want to look closer. The posts are stock fare but are trimmed with trellis grids that add visual texture as well as support for climbing plants. Curved braces create the suggestion of an arch, but the four straight beams actually create the overhead connection. Because there's much more material than is structurally necessary, it's obvious that the arbor itself is meant to be showcased as much as any plants it supports.

In fact with an arbor this beautiful, it would be a shame to let the vines get too lush and obscure it.

Although arbors can vary dramatically, this one has the quintessential arched doorway and latticework that give it highly traditional beauty.

CONSTRUCTING THE CLASSIC ARBOR

This arbor has beautifully fitted joinery at the top that is a little complicated to build but will last for years if not decades.

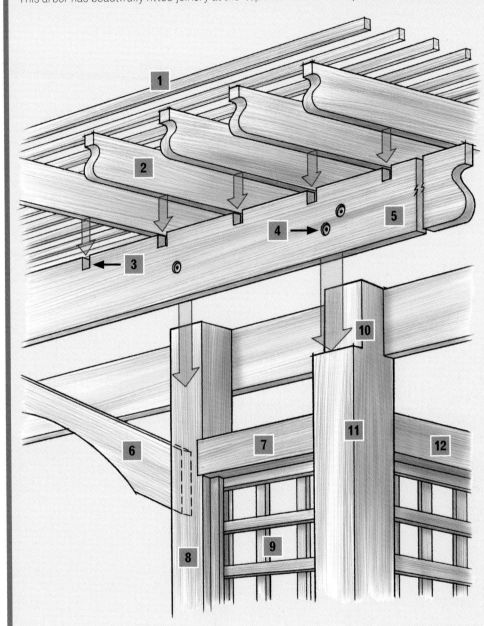

1. 1×2 lath, cut to 10 feet; 6 inches on center
2. 2×6 joists
3. Notches 1½ inches wide by 2 inches deep; 12 inches on center
4. Counterbore for lag screws
5. 2×10 beams, 12 feet long (4 pieces)
6. 2×6 knee braces (4 pieces)
7. 4×4 side rails, 15½ inches long (8 pieces)
8. 4×4 center posts (4 pieces)
9. Trellis infill made from 1×2 stock; grid openings approximately 4 inches
10. 7-inch-long tenon at post top
11. 6×6 corner posts (4 pieces)
12. 4×4 end rails, 25 inches long (4 pieces)

- Decide on an anchoring technique for the arbor (see page 25) and install concrete footings to attach at least the four 6×6 corner posts.
- Paint or stain the lumber as desired before cutting individual parts; later apply paint to notches, cut ends, and any other exposed surfaces.
- Cut tenons on the corner post upper ends as shown, then cut 4×4 rails and 1×2 stock for trim and trellises to connect the posts for each base half. This includes the side sections with the 4×4 posts.
- Cut four 2×10 beams to length and scroll-cut the ends as shown. Also cut notches along the upper beam edges as shown.

- Attach the two base assemblies to their footings, checking that each is plumb and correctly aligned. Before final tightening or installation of hardware, fit the four beams in place and recheck alignment of the post assemblies. Clamp temporarily, then drill and install bolts as shown.
- Cut 2×6 joists to length and scroll-cut the ends as shown; nest the joists inside the beam notches and secure with galvanized nails or deck screws.
- Cut and attach 1×2 lath on top of the joist edges as shown; secure with galvanized nails or deck screws.

GARDEN STRUCTURES BUILDING TECHNIQUES

When building the classic arbor on pages 89–90, the following techniques will make the process go smoother and faster and give you more uniform results. These are techniques that are also useful in building a number of other structures in the book. And even if you don't end up building the structure yourself, it's useful to understand them so you can go over them as your garden structure is built and make sure the best techniques are used.

How to Cut a Tenon. A mortise-and-tenon joint is one of the strongest, most stable joints you can make. Here's how to do it on the large scale necessary for most garden structures.

Step 1: After setting the saw's cutting depth to 1 inch (make a test cut to confirm; don't rely on the saw guide scale), clamp an angle square to the post to guide the first cut for the tenon shoulder.

Step 2: Next make a series of freehand cuts at the same depth, spaced no more than ½ inch apart, across the remaining "waste" area. This will leave a section of thin "fins" that will break off easily. Then flip the post over and repeat steps 1 and 2 for the opposite face.

Step 3: Use a wood chisel and/or hammer to break away the fins from the tenon. The remaining surface will be slightly rough, but you'll clean that up in the next step.

Step 4: To fit properly the tenon's faces, called cheeks, must be smooth. Use a coarse file called a wood rasp to scrape off any ridges or high spots; the saw cut lines will act as a depth guide. Repeat on the opposite cheek then repeat the cutting and filing process for the remaining corner posts.

How to Gang-Cut Notches. The classic arbor requires several notches made in a very uniform manner, as do a number of larger structures. Here's how to make such notches quickly and efficiently.

Step 1: The center posts need a shallow notch in one face to accept the crossbraces. Reset the saw cut depth to ¼ or ½ inch then make the two outer scoring cuts with the help of an angle square guide.

Step 2: With the two outer guided cuts made, make a series of freehand scoring cuts spaced about ¼ inch apart. Note that this technique is similar to that used for the tenons on the corner posts, but here the posts are clamped together with ends aligned. Called gang-cutting, this method is faster than notching each post individually.

Step 3: The shallow depth of cut in these notches means the scrap "fins" don't break off as easily; instead use a sharp wood chisel to make paring cuts as shown to remove the waste wood. If necessary follow up with a rasp to smooth the surface.

How to Cut a Decorative Edge. The classic arbor has lovely embellishments at the ends of its crossbeams. These embellishments are also often used on trellises and pergolas. They're easy to make and you can even design your own. Here are the basics.

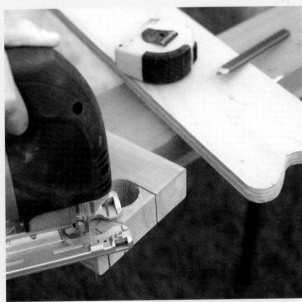

Step 1: For the decorative shape on the joist ends, make a pattern out of plywood and trace the outline on each joist. Drill a hole to create the inside arc of the curve as shown.

Step 2: Use the jigsaw to finish cutting the end profile. First make a few relief cuts into the end so waste portions can drop away, then cut along the traced outline on the surface.

Arbors With Gates

Add a gate to an arbor and you have charm that is nothing less than storybook. And since arbors are often used as an entrance or to mark the beginning of a pathway, gates combined with arbors are also practical.

Take your cue for the height of the gate from surrounding structures and fences. If the arbor is attached to privacy fencing, it makes sense to make the gate as high as the fencing. If the arbor is attached to a low or picket fence, a gate at that same lower height would be right.

If the arbor has nothing on either side of it—it's straddling a path or is otherwise out in the open—a gate would probably look out of place.

Unless you are trying to make a deliberate architectural statement with a tall solid slab, keep the upper portion of the "door" slightly open by using a screen, trellis grid, lattice, or some other see-through feature. In most cases you'll want to maintain the sight line so the open effect of the arbor is still intact; fitting it with a solid door closes the view and can make the garden area seem smaller.

As for stylistic details, aim for consistency with the arbor and any attached structures such as trellises rather than architectural elements of the house. This is especially true for arbors that are placed in the middle of the garden, well away from the house. Keep the scale, materials, details, and color of the gate fairly consistent with the rest of the arbor unless you are deliberately seeking contrast or an eclectic look.

In most cases it's best to treat the gate as another design element, another opportunity for an accent that makes the garden more interesting. This applies even if the gate has a specific function, such as keeping pets or small children from wandering out of the yard.

Most gates on arbors are built as part of the overall design. If you want to add a gate after an arbor is built, it will probably be next to impossible to find just the right one prebuilt. Most arbor gates that are added after the fact are made-to-spec jobs.

TIPS FOR GATED ARBORS

- Design the arbor with enough stability to handle the extra weight of a gate and shifting momentum as the gate opens and closes. You may have to use thicker posts, and you'll likely have to reinforce attachments to heavier concrete footings.

- Plan your gate design and operation to avoid obstructions. The bottom of the gate should be high enough to easily clear any existing or planned paving or pathways. It should also be able to clear plants or hardscape features such as inground lighting or small boulders. On sloped sites be sure the gate swings toward the downhill side of the arbor.

- Use large-scale hardware designed especially for gates. Bigger fasteners allow easier operation with gloved hands and reduce potentially tight clearances that might pinch a finger.

- Install a return spring or self-closing hinges so the gate will close and latch by itself when released. Left to swing freely the gate might sustain damage in high winds.

Even with dense plantings and tall lattice panels flanking it, this arbor still needs a gate to make the backyard private. Notice that the view is never blocked entirely, only filtered.

Aside from functioning to close off a pathway when necessary, a gate can add more substance to the look of an arbor. By itself this modest arbor sports a graceful arch and trellis side panels that make it appealing, but it would seems a little lightweight without a gate. The gate brings some solidity to the lower half, making the entire structure more substantial.

Some gates stop you in your tracks both figuratively and literally. This impressively crafted cedar gate is handsome enough to make you forget that it also serves a functional role.

Arbors With Gates

When your arbor will be positioned between a public and a private space, a gate makes even more sense. For one thing a gate adds security, even if it's just a psychological deterrent to someone entering your backyard. It makes a visitor or neighborhood kid pause before coming in, and it also sets a boundary for children and pets that need to stay in the safety of an enclosed yard.

In many of these situations, maintaining visibility beyond the gate isn't as important as when the arbor is situated in the middle of a garden. Instead the need for increased privacy might dictate a taller or solid gate that wouldn't seem appropriate in a more casual setting.

A gate adds another layer of structure to an arbor, nudging it away from a purely decorative role and more into one as a functional structure. For this reason you should plan on more custom work and more deliberate design choices if a gated arbor is intended as an extension of the home into its outdoor areas. Repetition of colors or key architectural details is the simplest way to make this connection. A gated arbor often provides the opportunity to add more colors or features, the way a house facade typically has layers of siding, window trim, and accents to add interest. Look for opportunities to incorporate or mimic these elements in your gate design.

Keep in mind that while immediate proximity to a home calls for most garden structures to be stylistically compatible with the host building, it doesn't always require an exact match. Aim for a resemblance that a first-time visitor would recognize and details that seem appropriate to the surroundings.

Painted the same color as the home's front door, this arbor gate leaves no doubt that it performs a similar role for the outdoor area. It is the entry to the home's private outdoor space.

Asian-Inspired Arbors

So what makes an arbor Asian inspired? Just as there is no single European or American architectural style, Asian design elements come from diverse sources and have evolved over time. Still there are signature elements that designers rely on to create that unmistakable flavor of the Far East.

For starters the framework tends to consist of a few large timbers rather than many smaller components. The joinery, often complex and ornate, is meant to be seen and admired rather than covered with trim or molding. The geometry is simple with few curved parts and no elaborate scrollwork save for carved rafter ends or curled roof trim. Horizontal lines sometimes step upward in small increments, creating a subtle arching effect called a cloud lift. Grids are commonly square rather than diamond shaped.

The finish tends to be minimal: either a subtle earth tone or gray from natural weathering or a single color such as a bright red or deep green.

It's also notable that Asian philosophy calls for the gardener to observe the site carefully and design an arbor in harmony with the site rather than altering the site to work with the structure.

Keep in mind your overall garden design and region when considering an Asian-style arbor. It would look drastically out of place in, say, a cottage garden with lots of white latticework. But it might appear very much at home in a restrained garden of alpines.

Asian design is a transplant that can look odd in the Deep South or on a Midwestern prairie. But in such an area as the Pacific Northwest, with its ties to the Far East, Asian design seems to fit in comfortably, especially in the landscape of a home with modern or Asian elements.

Pegged mortise-and-tenon joinery reveals hints of Asian influence in this arbor-and-trellis structure. Grids made of bamboo, often used as an accent material, reinforce the Asian feel.

This arbor blends a subtle mix of Asian-inspired touches but has no dominant stylistic theme. Large timbers make up the frame, square grid panels fill in the gates, and the curved knee braces create a cloud-lift effect where they meet the beams overhead.

Asian-Inspired Arbors

Asian arbors are distinctive in design and materials as well as in construction techniques. With some designs the joinery and shaping of parts might involve handwork with unfamiliar tools, but compared to the ornate carving or complex geometry in typical Victorian designs, these methods and materials are much more user friendly. In fact anyone who can tie a shoelace already has a grasp on one of the most common traditional techniques for attaching a structure's parts—tying them with rope or reeds.

Tying is especially useful for joining bamboo components. Their irregular shapes and brittle surfaces often split when they encounter metal fasteners, and lashing also looks more authentic. Wood posts and beams often feature mortise-and-tenon joinery secured with wood pegs. You can substitute screws and bolts in some cases, but try to keep modern metal hardware out of sight.

Though it's flanked by ornately carved fence panels and is fitted with matching gates, this Asian-inspired arbor boasts a classically simple form.

BUILDING AN ASIAN-STYLE ARBOR

The key to this Asian arbor is the joinery at the top and the position of the purlins.

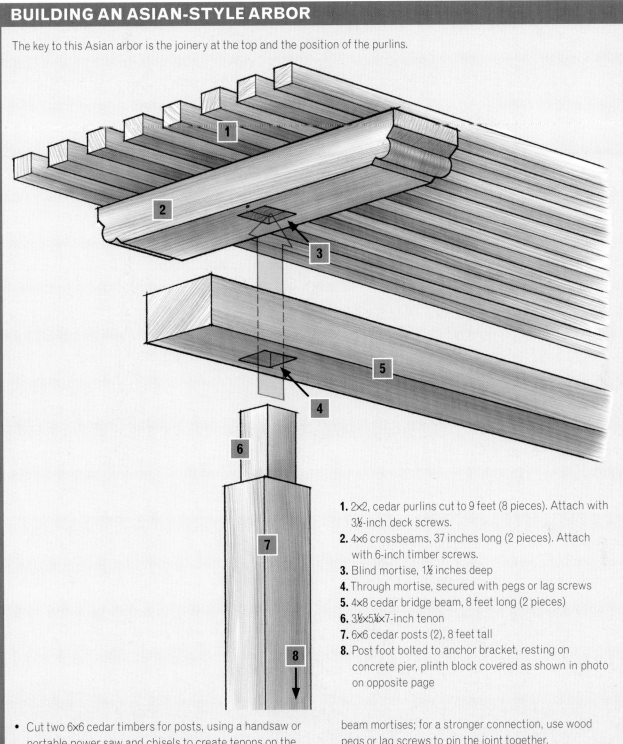

1. 2×2, cedar purlins cut to 9 feet (8 pieces). Attach with 3½-inch deck screws.
2. 4×6 crossbeams, 37 inches long (2 pieces). Attach with 6-inch timber screws.
3. Blind mortise, 1½ inches deep
4. Through mortise, secured with pegs or lag screws
5. 4×8 cedar bridge beam, 8 feet long (2 pieces)
6. 3½×5¼×7-inch tenon
7. 6×6 cedar posts (2), 8 feet tall
8. Post foot bolted to anchor bracket, resting on concrete pier, plinth block covered as shown in photo on opposite page

- Cut two 6×6 cedar timbers for posts, using a handsaw or portable power saw and chisels to create tenons on the upper ends.
- Secure the lower ends of the posts to concrete footings by bolting them to metal post base hardware. To camouflage the hardware, use finish nails to attach carved plinth blocks at the post bases, as shown in the photograph on the opposite page.
- Check the posts for plumb and realign if necessary. Then use a drill and wide wood chisel to cut a pair of through mortises in a 4x8 bridge beam as shown, with the beam oriented flat. The post tenons will extend through the

beam mortises; for a stronger connection, use wood pegs or lag screws to pin the joint together.
- Use a handsaw and plane to shape the crossbeam ends as illustrated and cut a shallow mortise in the underside of the beams as shown. Use long timber screws to attach the crossbeams to the bridge beam.
- Mill 4x4 cedar post stock to make eight purlins measuring 2½ inches square in cross section. Drill pilot holes and attach the purlins to the crossbeams as shown using long deck screws.
- Apply a clear penetrating sealer to help protect the wood against water and harsh weather.

Arbors With Seating

A well-designed arbor makes you want to linger awhile, and if the arbor happens to have a seat that lets you do just that, so much the better.

Doorway-type arbors encourage passing through but this type of arbor typically is larger (usually twice as wide) with a more substantial roof to encourage you to sit down in comfort. And since most arbors are built to allow vines to scramble over them, you can also enjoy the cool shade, foliage, and flowers while you relax.

The simplest option is probably to build a flat bench across the arbor, which has the benefit of further stabilizing the structure.

A prefabricated bench also will fit nicely into most arbors. Make sure the footing is relatively firm or the bench is certain to sink into soft ground and become an uneven, unstable perch. Often well-established, thick grass will do but you may need to add pavers or flagstone.

Swings are another popular option under arbors. However since they need to carry a lot of weight (at least 400 pounds) that's in motion, the arbor must be sturdy.

Like any other outdoor structures, seating arbors can vary from dirt simple to highly elaborate. This rustic version emphasizes a no-fuss approach to enjoying the garden.

Whether you call this attractive structure an arbor or a pergola, it's sturdy enough to support a porch swing. The design could get away with just two support posts but instead uses four, which gives it visual substance. Also because the two outer posts are well away from the swing, there's no worry about branches and thorns getting in the way.

Whether the site for a quiet conversation or some well-deserved solitude, a seating arbor like this creates its own mini environment. Wrapped in lush ivy and flowering vines, it conveys a genuine sense of shelter.

Built-in seating can add charm and function to an arbor but shouldn't interfere with foot traffic through the garden. This arbor is unusually and distinctively wide, leaving plenty of room for simple plank benches that allow foot traffic through and also allow the arbor to serve as a small gathering space.

As arbors gain seating or other features, they start to blur the line between the different kinds of garden structures. This one has the small scale of an arbor along with trellises to support vines, but its design suggests a pergola.

Arbors With Seating

Adding seating to an arbor is a lovely way to get more use out of the arbor. Not only is it pleasant to look at but you can also relax under it.

An arbor with seating must be designed and positioned in a way so there's adequate clearance for people, wheelbarrows, and the like to pass by after a bench is installed. Make sure there's at least 4 feet of pathway. And if the path is going to be used more than occasionally, more than 4 feet.

Another concern is structural balance and weight distribution. For built-in benches, suspended swings, and any other seating that is supported directly by the arbor, make sure the posts, beams, and other structural components are of sufficient size and grade to carry the extra weight. Keep in mind that you are adding the weight of the bench or swing—and of the people using it.

Swinging benches also require that the arbor posts be securely anchored to the ground or that the structure have a low center of gravity that prevents it from tipping over from the swing's momentum. If these basic precautions are taken, you can enjoy your arbor in the carefree way intended.

Tucked away in its own private alcove, this arbor and bench ensemble is a prime spot to relax, but it also provides a strong focal point in the garden's design. Imagine how bland the scene would look without it.

Arbors as Front Entries

Since arbors are like doorways, what could be more appropriate than using one as an outdoor front entry?

An arbor leading into a front yard adds charm and invites visitors to come through—a signal that you care enough about the outside world and visitors to take extra care in making their journey to your front door a pleasant one.

Instead of beckoning people an arbor can create a desirable barrier between your front yard and the wider world. In a densely populated neighborhood or on a small lot in an urban setting, an arbor can serve as an informal guardian, especially if it's fitted with a gate. Typically an arbor provides no real security unless it's flanked by a tall fence and built with features that make unauthorized entry difficult. Still it can act as a buffer to street and local pedestrian traffic, offering a little more privacy than the yard would otherwise enjoy.

SMART DESIGN FOR AN ENTRY ARBOR

- Make it tall enough: Arbors should be about 76 inches high to accommodate taller people. If you plan to have vines overhead, allow another 4 to 6 inches since shoots will twine underneath and hang down.
- Make it wide enough: Allow at least 3 feet to accommodate one person easily. If you'd like two people to pass through (and want to give a feeling of generous hospitality), make the arbor 4 to 5 feet across.
- Repeat a trim color or prominent architectural feature from the house to ensure the arbor looks compatible.
- Isolated arbors look as awkward in front yards as they do in backyards; combine the arbor with planters, a fence, or other landscape features so it doesn't look as though it were dropped haphazardly onto the site.
- Never rest a freestanding arbor on the ground without anchoring it securely. Use concrete footings or other means to ensure wind or passersby won't inadvertently topple the structure (see page 25).
- If installing a gate, mount it so it swings in toward the yard, not out toward a public sidewalk. Install hardware so the gate is either latched shut or held fully open; allowing a gate to swing freely invites wind damage as well as potential injury to people.

With its white painted finish and arched profile, this arbor mimics the home's front entry, a smart design trick that elongates the walk, making the front yard seem larger and giving a unified feel to the landscape and architecture.

Climbing roses add a vivid burst of color to the crisp white woodwork of this gated arbor and fence. In older or historic neighborhoods where homes sit near the street, features like this can make the most of a small front yard and buffer street noise.

Standing up front like a sentry, this arbor features a gable roof and strut frame that clearly establish its ties to the house in the background. Notice that the roof angle and style, but not the trim color, are repeated—and that's plenty to make the connection.

Arbors as Front Entries

Any garden structure on your property should be visually compatible with your home, but with a front entry arbor it's critical. After all the arbor will become something of a lens through which your home is viewed.

Look for cues from your house when designing or selecting an entry arbor. First and foremost is style: An ornate Victorian arbor would look silly in front of a sleek midcentury ranch home, and so would an Asian-inspired bamboo arbor in front of a Dutch colonial.

Try to echo basic building materials, architectural details, and finishes such as paint color. Look for elements from the house to work into the arbor. For example if there's a front or side fence consider making the arbor part of that and use the style of the fence as inspiration for the style of the arbor.

When you're building from a kit and have limited control over the style of the arbor, look for embellishments that will tie it into your home. You could paint the arbor a color that's on the home. Or if there's terracing perhaps incorporate the arbor into the terraces.

When the pathway to the front door leads from the driveway or garage area, think about using a short length of fence or latticework to visually as well as literally tie the arbor to the garage or house.

Aim for an arbor that looks as if it was designed and built at the same time and in the same manner as your house, not one that was constructed long afterward. You'll achieve a visual harmony that will truly be welcoming.

Arbors and other outdoor structures are so often associated with traditional home styles that it's easy to forget their value in contemporary designs. Here a gated arbor provides privacy and ornament to a modern home that would likely seem stark and exposed without it.

Arbors With Fences

Combining an entry arbor with a fence is a great way to get the most out of both.

Since the arbor is a doorway, the fence serves as walls and directs foot traffic right to the opening. And when movement through the garden is clearly directed in this manner, it helps the design feel right.

A fence also helps to make an arbor seem more substantial and more logically positioned. It visually anchors an arbor, which can look a little lonely if it's put in the middle of an open space.

There's also a botanical bonus to a fence. If you're growing vines on the arbor, the fence also can serve as support for the vines, especially wide-spreading ones that can roam 20 feet or more.

If privacy is your goal, a tall fence can provide that. But tall fences can feel oppressive or unfriendly, and an arbor can fix that so you have the best of both worlds—a little privacy but also a limited invitation for people to come on in and enjoy your landscape with you.

For an arbor it pays to have connections. This simple arched version gains stature from its trellis and vines and also because a matching grid fence tethers it to the house. Those elements give the structure more substance and create a small alcove for plants.

By closing off some of the view in a garden, fences attached to arbors direct your eye to the central opening—namely the arbor itself. This gracefully arched arbor and its flanking display platforms are all the more dramatic because the latticework fence provides a backdrop.

None of the usual reasons for a fence would warrant a design as open as this one, which provides virtually no privacy and wouldn't do much to keep pets from straying. But as an aesthetic companion to an impressive arbor, the fence strikes a nice balance and lets the arbor keep its starring role.

Arbors With Fences

When planning the design of your arbor combined with a fence, make sure that they are compatible in both function and appearance.

Keep the fence's prominence secondary to the arbor itself, even if it means compromising a bit on its function. A tall solid mass of imposing wood panels is likely to create a fortresslike appearance that overpowers any grace the arbor might have contributed to the garden. You can choose from plenty of fence designs that yield a lighter and more open look but still create an effective enclosure if that's necessary. Lattice panels are a perennial favorite though certainly aren't the only option. Consider also lattice or other openwork at the top of a tall, solid fence.

A companion fence doesn't need to literally connect to the arbor, but the two should look as though they go together. A shared color is one way to prevent too much contrast, which will tend to make the structures look mismatched. If the arbor has an arched top or bridge, keep the fence height limited to the base of the arch or find a way to introduce a complementary curve or angle where the fence meets the arbor.

This fence not only visually anchors the elaborate arbor in the space, it also helps screen the view and provides some privacy. Note that the design of the fence echoes many of the details of the arbor.

Apertures in Arbors

Latticework is charming, but when you have a large expanse of it, it starts looking a bit stark. A great solution to this situation is to include a windowlike opening—a circle, an oval, a half circle, a diamond, a rectangle, or a square.

Among design and engineering folks, these openings are called apertures. Sometimes they have a literal or practical function, such as allowing movement or providing ventilation. Other times they are aesthetic features meant to break up a solid wall or allow a view, and these properties make them useful and appealing in garden arbors.

Creating an aperture in an arbor typically involves cutting and then trimming an opening in solid or lattice-weave panels that make up portions of the sidewalls.

Apertures are especially simple to include when they are shaped by straight lines, as with a square. Curved or circular openings are trickier to create, but offer a welcome contrast to the straight lines and angles typically found in the lattice framework.

The circular windowlike opening in this arbor panel adds interest with its contrasting shape and also allows more enjoyment of the garden itself by offering a view. Simple apertures such as this can be used to keep structures from feeling too enclosed or blocking sight lines into the yard.

INCORPORATING AN APERTURE

Creating an opening in lath is not hard. This one is created by routing out two rings of ½-inch CDX plywood and screwing them onto the lath. Then use a jigsaw to rough-cut just inside the plywood rings.

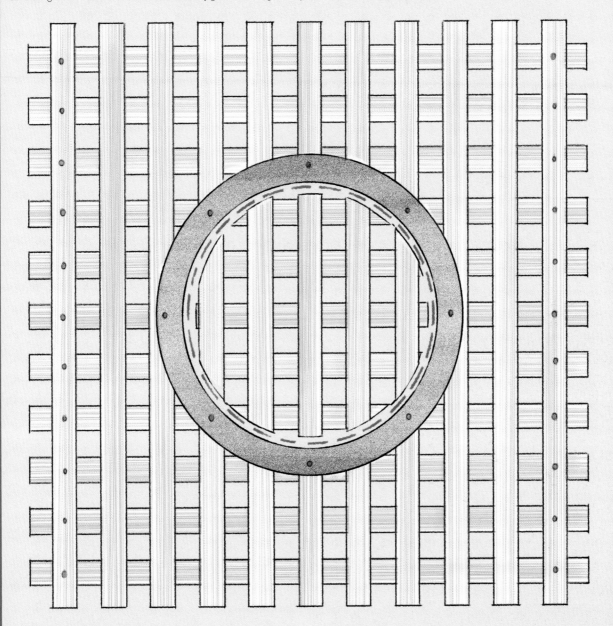

1. Use a yardstick and pencil to fashion a simple compass or find round objects you can trace (you'll need one smaller and one larger circle, for marking the inside and outside diameters of the trim ring).

2. Determine where you want to create an aperture and mock up a cardboard cutout to simulate the size and placement. Try to balance the grid pattern around the opening, leaving similar patterns of partially covered grid squares.

3. Mark the outlines for two trim rings on a sheet of exterior-grade plywood (½ inch or thicker). Cut along the lines with a portable jigsaw, or for more precise shapes use a router with a trammel guide to cut the circles.

4. Sand the trim rings to remove splinters and sharp edges, then prime and paint or apply a solid-color exterior stain.

5. Clamp the trim rings on opposite sides of the lattice panel and align them, then use screws to fasten them. Place screws at overlap joints to penetrate both layers of the lattice.

6. Use a jigsaw to cut away the lattice material just inside the trim rings. Sand any protruding stubs flush with the trim rings or remove them with a router and flush-trim bit. Touch up the paint or stain on the lattice panel.

The length and stature of a tunnel arbor make the journey through one seem almost like a procession. Under this graceful arched iron arbor, that sense of anticipation is rewarded with a secluded sitting area. A strong connection to other landscape features is essential for a tunnel arbor because it creates a feeling of expectation.

Tunnel Arbors

Ever since Monet began painting his beautiful allée at Giverny, gardeners worldwide have fallen in love with tunnel arbors.

A tunnel arbor is just what it sounds like, a larger and longer cousin of the simple arches and gateways seen on the preceding pages. This type of arbor is most often seen in a large public or estate garden, but it really adds drama and stature to an otherwise ordinary private yard.

A natural form of a tunnel arbor can be found in the allée, which consists of parallel rows of trees straddling a path or even a country lane, with a broad leafy canopy arching overhead from both sides to provide shade. That's fine if you have a decade or more to wait for trees to mature, but you can achieve a similar effect with a built arbor. Fortunately with a tunnel arbor vines will fill in overhead in just two or three years.

Like their smaller relatives tunnel arbors need a context,

a landscape containing other features that the structure complements or enhances. Stick one out in the open and it tends to look odd. It conveys a sense of movement, the feeling that you travel through rather than to it. Thus the shape is long and somewhat narrow, and it typically connects to some defining feature or marker at the end—a courtyard, a gate to another outdoor space, or perhaps a formal garden with a fountain.

And while the more dramatic tunnel arbors need a lot of space, a modest version can fit even in a limited space. Try one in a side yard or along the back of your property.

Unlike some garden structures designed to stay exposed, tunnel arbors are often built as scaffolding that disappears under the foliage of plants they support. This inexpensive version of a tunnel arbor is fashioned from plastic plumbing pipe arches and horizontal wood lath braces. Climbing roses have clambered up its sides.

Tunnel Arbors

When planning a tunnel arbor, keep in mind some design basics. Each pair of supporting posts represents a station; combine at least three stations to create a length of no less than 8 or 10 feet (more if you have room). These multiple stations, connected by overhead beams or purlins, tend to pull your gaze incrementally through the structure. Instead of looking past the arbor to the other end, you look through it; it's part of the view you get to enjoy.

The other key to successful arbor design is to avoid making the structure feel too closed in, especially if your view is blocked at eye level. Low plants or half-walls along the pathway are fine, and coverage overhead will merely suggest shelter. But make it too enclosed and it's going to feel claustrophobic and unpleasant—the last sensation you want a garden structure to create. So from waist height up to about 6 feet or so, leave plenty of open area.

Remember tall people too. You'll want a person well over 6 feet to be able to walk through easily, so shoot for a height of at least 6½ feet at the structure's highest point. That will allow for taller visitors and for vines to droop down somewhat.

Tunnel arbors can be fashioned from wood, but metal versions tend to have a lighter look and can incorporate curves and other design flourishes more easily. Your average carpenter won't be able to help you here; check business directory listings for local metal fabricators (or suppliers they might frequent), especially artisans who do more residential than industrial work.

Prominent structural elements like these round columns and thick connecting beams create a strong sense of enclosure even though this arbor features wide open bays. Each column and beam is a momentary focal point that helps create a dramatic tunnel effect.

This contemporary-looking tunnel arbor, situated next to the house and sharing its stucco finish and trim colors, has more architectural presence than a typical garden structure. Leaving the bays largely open does nothing to dilute the sense of structure, and it leaves room for potted flowers that brighten the pathway.

Arbors on Pedestals

Arbor posts are often anchored to low concrete footings or sometimes are simply embedded directly into the ground (something that should be done only with pressure-treated lumber, the most rot-resistant wood choice). These simple methods are fine for small outdoor structures, but with more substantial structures you'll need something sturdier.

Brick or stone pedestals are more permanent. They keep wood posts away from ground moisture, and the masonry provides contrast and interest. If your home has any masonry features—brick or stone siding, foundation facing, planters, or other accents—repeating the material in the arbor pedestals is an ideal way to seamlessly incorporate the arbor into its setting.

These pedestals are made from plywood faced with shake shingles. Especially with all-wood construction such as this, the spaces around the post have to be well-designed and sealed with caulk to prevent water seepage.

Pedestals for pergolas and other outdoor structures can be made from a variety of materials. These have concrete centers faced with brick.

BUILDING A MASONRY PEDESTAL

Like most foundation supports, pedestals fare better when they sit on a wide and sturdy concrete footing. In northern regions where winter freezing can cause frost heave, structural footings typically penetrate below the frost line. That's always a good idea, but it's not always necessary with arbors and other small, simple structures.

In the same way that small concrete slabs can "float" on the moving soil, there's typically enough flexibility in an arbor frame to withstand some minor movement if the footings rise and settle independently of each other. If you dig down through the top soil at least 1 or 2 feet and compact some crushed rock in the hole to allow drainage, you'll likely render most frost disturbances insignificant. If you don't want to take a chance, go to the frost line and pour a taller footing for your pedestal.

For a wraparound pedestal like the one shown here, mortar the stone or brick in an alternating pinwheel pattern so the corners overlap from one course to the next. When the mortar has set firmly (at least 24 hours) you can fit the arbor post in place and fill the center core with concrete. For the top course of brick or stone, leave a slight gap (about ⅛ inch) to allow for post movement and swelling; fill the gap with a flexible exterior caulk.

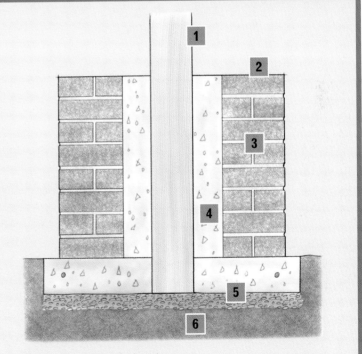

1. 4x4 pressure-treated post
2. 3-inch stone or brick cap
3. 6x8x6 cut stone or concrete block
4. Concrete fill
5. Concrete footing with ½-inch rebar
6. Compacted crushed stone

Creating Curved-Top Arbors

Whether it's a towering half-round arch or a low and subtle eyebrow shape, a curved top brings personality and style to an arbor. Curved construction also makes the structure a little more unusual and says quality craftsmanship in a way few other architectural details can.

Arches do take more time and skill than, say, straight crossbeams but their charm more than makes up for the extra effort.

When designing with curves, it's especially effective if you can echo other curves in the landscape or hardscape, such as a curve in a sidewalk or patio pavers laidout in a circular pattern.

You have a number of different options for creating a curved shape in wood. Shown here are three especially attractive methods: cutting the piece from a single wide board (see page 150), stack laminating thick boards and cutting the curve from the glued rough blank, or making a bentwood lamination from flexible strips of wood.

The stack lamination method is explained here, and the bentwood lamination method on page 120. Choose the best one for your project.

The arch on this classic small arbor is a deliberate focal point, creating a lighter and more ornamental look than a flat top.

The massive size of this arbor requires an equally massive arch. This one is constructed by stacking sturdy pieces of lumber atop each other, screwing them together, and then cutting out the arch.

CONSTRUCTING A STACK LAMINATE ARCH

This method uses milled 2× or thicker lumber edge glued in a stepped or offset pattern as seen in the illustration. The exact gluing pattern is determined by the arch contours, indicated by the dashed lines. In this example the elongated ends allow for a footed design with a decorative detail.

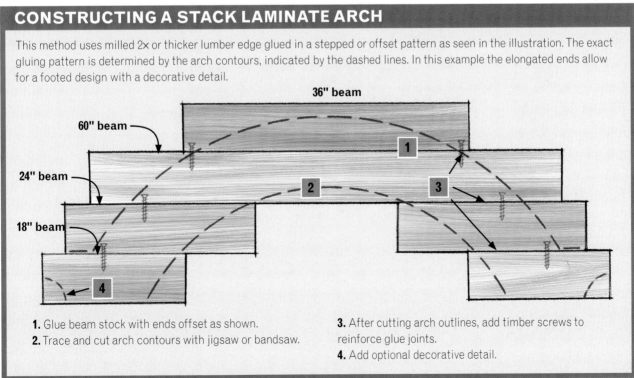

36" beam
60" beam
24" beam
18" beam

1
2
3
4

1. Glue beam stock with ends offset as shown.
2. Trace and cut arch contours with jigsaw or bandsaw.

3. After cutting arch outlines, add timber screws to reinforce glue joints.
4. Add optional decorative detail.

CONSTRUCTING A BENTWOOD LAMINATE ARCH

Segmented arches and curves work fine for many arbors, but other techniques are better suited if the scale gets larger or the curve contour is more elaborate. A bentwood lamination, small or large, is relatively easy to make with help from a simple shop-built jig.

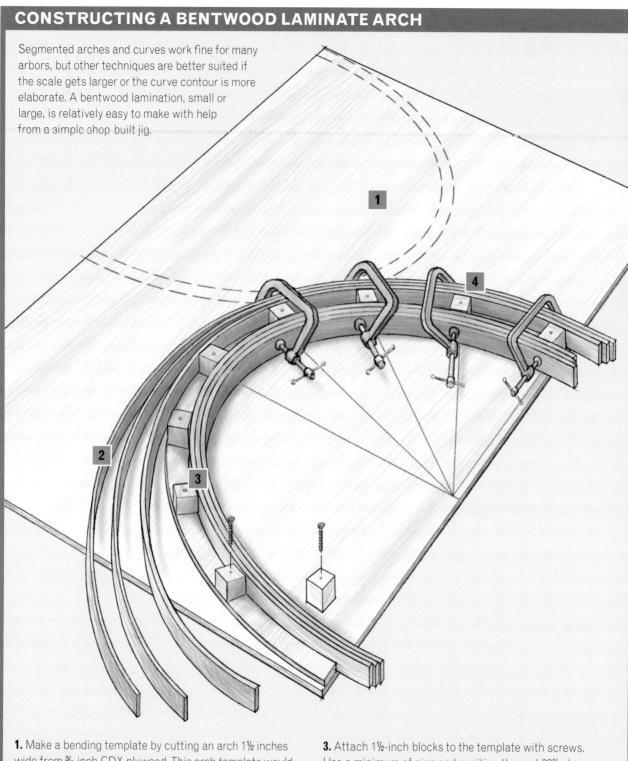

1. Make a bending template by cutting an arch 1½ inches wide from ¾-inch CDX plywood. This arch template would measure 55½ inches across from the inside of the arch to 27¾ high on the inside of the arch. Repeat for a second arch template.

2. Create the top and bottom of each arch with ¼-inch bender board, available in 3- and 4-inch widths. (Cut on a tablesaw to desired width.)

Glue together three layers of the bender board for a total of four long, narrow pieces for the project.

3. Attach 1½-inch blocks to the template with screws. Use a minimum of nine and position them at 22½-degree intervals as shown. Repeat with the second template.

4. Bend a piece of the bentwood along the outside and inside of the arch template as shown. Start on one end and work your way along the arch, clamping at each spot where there is a block.

After the glue dries, cut the ends of each arch flush.

This curved-top arbor features arch sets (one lower/inner and one upper/outer) bent-laminated from thin wood strips. The arch sets are connected with 2×2 rungs attached with deck screws.

Rustic Arbors

Especially in a country or wooded landscape, rustic arbors made of sturdy branches with the bark still intact add a naturalistic charm. It's a style especially popular in Western settings as well.

This style, often called live branch, has many advantages. First, if you have a ready supply of timber, you can get your materials free and have the the satisfaction of harvesting what is handy. Also the construction techniques are simple as are the tools needed for these projects (see page 124).

The live-branch arbors shown here featuring whole tree branches and trunks are rustic at its most basic. No other technique creates a structure so at home in a wooded setting, because the logs and branches blend in as if they are still alive and growing.

Another type of rustic garden structure construction uses rough-sawn lumber, which is produced by a power-driven sawmill and has blade marks and other surface imperfections still visible. Sometimes the wood is shaped with axes and adzes, tools that leave a chiseled surface (See pages 30 to 31 for examples).

Rough construction such as live branch and rough-sawn have another advantage. Their rough surfaces are ideal for a wide variety of vines to grow up with little or sometimes no assistance from the gardener.

A jumble of roses and other flowers provides the perfect setting for this live-branch tunnel arbor. There's no attempt to mimic architectural elements here, just the structural basics required to hold the roof up and keep everything steady.

The use of rustic design and materials doesn't necessarily mean crude engineering. Both of these arbors feature curved roof structures that increase strength and exploit the tension inherent in the bent branches. In terms of efficiency, these techniques are actually smarter than using dressed lumber from milling machines.

Rustic Construction Techniques

The building of a live-branch structure starts with finding the wood. If you're lucky you'll have a ready supply of suitable materials right on your own land, or the land of friends or family.

If not, even city-dwellers shouldn't have to go far to locate materials. Tree-trimming services and utility maintenance crews generate large amounts of "waste" branches, especially in older urban neighborhoods with mature trees. Most of this material gets consigned to the chipper and the mulch pile. Find out if you can salvage usable branches when they are removing or trimming local trees, but don't expect work crews to interrupt their schedule or to take responsibility for your safety. In fact, some companies may have liability insurance coverage that prohibits non-employees from being on site during the job. If that's the case, simply ask them and/or the property owner to set aside some material for you to pick up later.

Whenever possible take advantage of the natural shapes and features of branches. Here the Y-shape end of this post cradles the beam branch as securely as any hand-cut joinery would.

BEST AND WORST WOODS FOR LIVE-BRANCH CONSTRUCTION

Good Woods: Willow (except weeping willow) is generally recognized as the premium species for making rustic bentwood projects, but the following woods also have good pliability and/or good weather resistance:
Alder
Cedar
Cypress
Dogwood
Juniper
Live oak
Locust
Viburnum
White oak

Poor Woods: Some woods bend poorly or tend to rot quickly when exposed to the elements.
Ash
Cherry
Maple
Pine
Red oak

Note: Redwood weathers well but cracks easily when bent. Use it for projects with no bending.

TIPS FOR LIVE-BRANCH CONSTRUCTION

- Try to work the wood immediately after harvesting, while it is still "green" and pliable with most of its original moisture content.
- If you want smooth branches with the bark stripped, harvest during the spring and summer, when the bark peels easily because of the moisture underneath. If you want the bark to stay on the branches, harvest branches during the winter when the bark's grip is more tenacious.
- A sharp hatchet, a handsaw, pruning shears, and a hammer and wood chisel set are the basic tools needed to craft most live-branch structures.
- For the best results use a cordless drill so you can make pilot holes and attach parts with screws or bolts; they hold better than nails.
- Green logs and branches have a high moisture content that can corrode metal hardware quickly. Whenever possible use hot-dipped galvanized or stainless-steel fasteners. Also use coarse-thread screws; they grip better.
- Smaller branches are better secured with wrapped wire than with fasteners, which tend to split narrow stock.
- If necessary soak branches in water and bend any that you want to shape into tight curves during the assembly process.
- Apply a low-sheen exterior varnish or sealer to protect the structure from moisture and decay and to make it last longer.

The smaller elements on this rustic arbor, such as the fan-shape trellis, often call for the bending of branches. For the arched overhead beams and other large structural elements, find branches that have a natural bend to them or use a highly flexible wood such as willow.

Smaller structures such as this twig trellis showcase the simplicity and character of live-branch construction. There are no critical engineering requirements here, so small branches and nailed joints work fine.

4 Pergolas

Imagine building the world's simplest room addition. The framework is basic, complicated utilities are nonexistent, and the windows, doors, and skylights are provided by nature.

Streamlined design lets you bypass siding, insulation, roofing, and a host of other expensive features. Granted, it's not exactly watertight or wind resistant, and it's a little shy on shelter during cold spells, but when the weather is fair you'd be hard pressed to find a better spot to relax or gather with friends or family.

Most versions offer shade to blunt the hot afternoon sun while allowing breezes to flow unimpeded. Pergolas also are fairly affordable and easy to build—you can put one together in a weekend or two. No wonder it's the most popular garden structure found anywhere.

It might seem odd that something this simple and spare could accomplish so much, but the pergola is versatile and it creates livable outdoor space at a fraction of the cost of an enclosed structure.

About Pergolas

What's the difference between an arbor and a pergola?

The answer may simply be personal interpretation. The terms are often used interchangeably. Both structures have open-top frames that may support climbing plants, and either can be paired with fences or trellises. But the similarities end there. Think about the difference between a miniature show pony and a large draft horse; the animals share a resemblance, but their roles are hardly identical.

As noted in the previous chapter, arbors tend to be relatively small or lightweight structures that mark an entrance or pathway. Some are gated and many feature arched tops or other ornamental elements, but most share that sense of being something you pass under as you move through a garden space. With a pergola there's little of that sense of movement. Instead its persona is more that of a shelter or gathering space, and it's usually big enough to enclose a seating group or a table and chairs for outdoor dining. Also arbors tend to have a closer relationship to the plants around them, including the vines they often support.

With the larger overall size of a pergola also comes a larger scale. Posts are typically 6x6 or larger timbers, and most of the other components are sized accordingly. Like arbors pergolas can be freestanding structures, but the Latin root of the word "pergula" means projecting roof, suggesting that early versions were attached to exterior walls and were used primarily to provide some relief from the sun.

Pergolas also have the added benefit of being somewhat evocative of their Mediterranean origins, especially of Italy. They create a romantic, charming space that most homeowners find hard to resist.

Remove the dining set from beneath this pergola, continue the patio area through to another area, and what do you have? An arbor. These subtle distinctions account for some of the blending of definitions of the two garden structures.

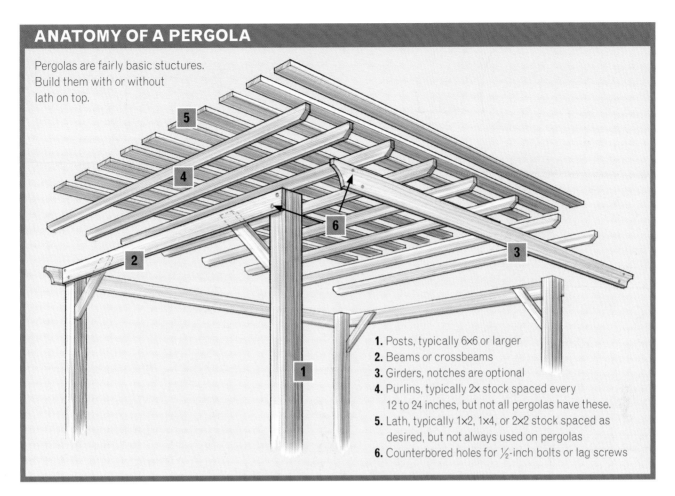

ANATOMY OF A PERGOLA

Pergolas are fairly basic stuctures. Build them with or without lath on top.

5

4

6

2

3

1

1. Posts, typically 6×6 or larger
2. Beams or crossbeams
3. Girders, notches are optional
4. Purlins, typically 2× stock spaced every 12 to 24 inches, but not all pergolas have these.
5. Lath, typically 1×2, 1×4, or 2×2 stock spaced as desired, but not always used on pergolas
6. Counterbored holes for ½-inch bolts or lag screws

Without this shallow pergola the French doors and back expanse of this house would seem a little stark. With it the space gains architectural detail and becomes an inviting nook.

This contemporary Southwestern pergola demonstrates how the right design and circumstances for an outdoor structure can add living space to a home. Repetition of the stucco and trim exterior makes for a smooth connection.

About Pergolas

Odds are your backyard has some sort of gathering place already—a patio or perhaps a deck—some space with room to set up a grill and a dining set or maybe a few Adirondack chairs.

Areas such as these can certainly be inviting and functional, but they tend to lack the definition and the presence that come with an overhead structure. Close them in too much, however, and you risk losing the direct connection to the open sky. When that happens there's little point to the outdoor space; it's merely become more enclosed square footage that keeps out the wind and rain. The goal is a space that connects you to the outdoors but doesn't leave you feeling exposed, and the difference between the two sensations can be surprisingly narrow.

Consider how your body reacts to temperature changes. At 70°F to 75°F/21°C to 24°C most people feel right at home, but push that dial ten degrees in either direction and comfort quickly gives way to a chill or a sweat. The ambience of an outdoor space can shift as easily.

Enter the pergola. This simple structure—consisting mostly of an open frame rather than solid surfaces—excels at striking a balance between your enjoyment of the outdoors and your instinctive need for shelter. The secret is the convincing suggestion of shelter, not necessarily the genuine article. Surrounded by hefty posts and beams, most people perceive the boundaries as comforting even if they aren't literal; a sudden downpour will soak you and wind gusts will peel the tablecloth, but unless either happens a pergola feels protective.

Some features, such as a shade-producing canopy, do offer real protection, but even without those amenities a pergola can do its job. More than anything else it signals that this space is set aside to enjoy.

This bare-bones pergola illustrates how the sense of shelter is nearly as effective as shelter itself. The dining area occupies a clearly defined space and invites people in despite the fact that literal protection from the elements is almost nonexistent.

A Classic Pergola

A well-designed pergola is deceptively elegant. By putting a few nice flourishes on a modest amount of standard lumber and assembling it in a fairly straightforward fashion, you will have a substantial structure to enclose an outdoor living or dining area

The secret to a well-designed classic pergola is in the scale and the flourishes. It needs to relate well to the landscape or any adjoining structure, repeating paint colors, architectural details, heights, and widths as much as possible.

The flourishes are simple but make it look like there's a lot going on architecturally. This pergola's joists have curved notches that add simple but striking detail. The structure is probably sturdy enough to stand on its own, but curved knee braces add another level of detail and craftsmanship.

This pergola is attached to a deck, but the design could easily be adapted to a freestanding pergola, anchored on concrete pier footings or a patio slab base.

Nestled close to the house but not attached to it, this deck-mounted pergola is part of a matching suite of outdoor structures that also includes a gated arbor and a seating arbor. The appearance of complexity comes from repetition of parts, not from a difficult design.

CONSTRUCTING THE CLASSIC PERGOLA

This project requires just a few sizes of western red cedar and relies on bolted connections and notched lap joinery to hold everything together.

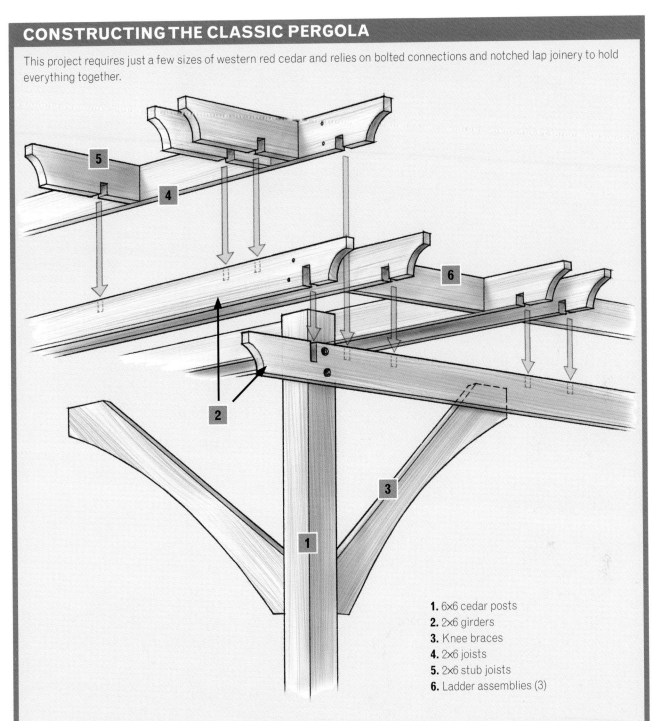

1. 6×6 cedar posts
2. 2×6 girders
3. Knee braces
4. 2×6 joists
5. 2×6 stub joists
6. Ladder assemblies (3)

- Cut four 9-foot posts from 6×6 cedar timbers. (Note: Post length and other dimensions can be adjusted as required for your site.)
- The overhead structure is simply a perimeter frame of 2×6 girders, capped by three ladder-type assemblies made of 2×6 joists and blocking. Two subassemblies with stub joists finish the sides.
- Cut notches where the joists and girders will overlap. The perimeter joists (at ends and sides) need half-depth notches (2¾ inches deep); the ladder and stub joists get shallower notches (2¼ inches).

- Establish the overall size of your pergola, then calculate the lengths and notch placement for various parts and make a sample of each. When you have the dimensions correct, make multiple versions.
- Stain or finish the precut parts before assembling the pergola. Recruit a helper or use temporary bracing to secure the posts into metal base brackets, then install the joist frame above. Finish by installing diagonal knee braces at each post.

Large enough to contain separate zones, this cedar pergola stretches nearly the full length of the house. Functioning as a true outdoor room, it has a massive brick fireplace at one end, a central dining area, and a small seating nook flanked by a patchwork frame of glass block inserts (at left).

Attached Pergolas

Aside from needing little in the way of materials, an attached pergola offers other advantages. Because the pergola relies on the solidity of the house frame, it requires less joinery and reinforcing hardware. An attached structure also delivers convenience. With indoor spaces just a few steps away, access to the kitchen or family room is quick, and it's easier to extend electrical lines from the house if you want lighting or other amenities. The pergola can add practical value by shading the house from the harshest sun—but not too much. You won't get as much shade as a solid roof might provide but if you train a deciduous vine on the pergola, you'll receive welcome shade in summer and equally welcome sun in winter.

An attached pergola provides a unique space for your home, a gathering place that is neither completely indoors nor out. It creates a transition between the two environments that takes something from each. Under the best circumstances this special ambience can lend a ritual quality to the time you spend there, especially if it involves meals and other gatherings with family and friends. The fact that such get-togethers are limited to fair weather simply makes them that much more appreciated.

With stately columns and crisp white paint to match the house trim, this pergola caps a masonry patio wall that makes the entire structure seem more substantial and permanent. Along with the surrounding trees, the pergola helps filter the sun streaming into the large window.

Attached Pergolas

An attached pergola functions as an extension of the house. It extends the living space out into the yard and serves as a graceful transition space between outdoors and indoors.

Attaching a pergola to a house is not difficult, but it does take a little knowledge of basic home construction. Most people are familiar with decks attached directly to the house; this construction method relies on a sturdy board (called a ledger) that is bolted to the home's rim joist, a solid section of the floor framing.

On multistory homes there's typically a second set of rim joists that help support the upper floor, and in those cases the pergola's top can often be attached much like a deck ledger board. Otherwise the pergola must be secured to wall studs, a window or door header, or other structural framing—never to the siding or sheathing alone.

The overhead part of a pergola doesn't have to stand up to the heavy loads that a deck must bear, but a collapse could easily cause serious injury or worse to people standing below.

Aside from technical requirements, consider how the pergola will extend from the house into the patio or garden area. The point of origin—typically over a sliding or French patio door or the exterior entry to the kitchen—is likely a given, so be sure the outward connection to the yard makes sense. Provide shelter for the patio area or direct the structure toward a planter area or perhaps a tree that can act as the outer focal point.

The second tier of this structure has been added for interest rather than strength. It also creates another layer of shade and produces interesting shadows.

There's no law that says the route from house to pergola has to be a straight line. The small porch overhang at the rear door branches sideways to an arbor, which in turn has an offset connection to the pergola. The result is much more unexpected and interesting than a direct attachment would be.

To establish a strong connection from an attached pergola to outlying garden areas, let climbing plants grow into the structure. Here a wisteria vine creates a dramatic canopy for the dining area.

Building Pergolas With Decks

Pergolas pair well with another outdoor structure designed to provide a gathering place—the universally popular backyard deck. If a pergola provides a ceiling, then a deck supplies a floor. A railing can serve as walls, if desired, to create the perfect outdoor room.

The affinity between decks and pergolas is all the more natural because they are often made from the same material—wood. This means the hardware and techniques translate seamlessly from one to another, making it easy to combine the structures when built simultaneously or when a pergola is retrofitted to an existing deck.

There's no need for identical materials however. In fact pergolas typically complement or match the house rather than mimic the details on a deck. The exception is a customized deck railing, but that feature is often patterned after the colors, materials, or architectural details of the house anyway.

A pergola doesn't have to contain the entire deck to create the ambience of an outdoor room. This view of the classic pergola project shown on page 133 reveals how the structure is perched on a part of the deck that serves as a cozy conversation area.

An exception to the rule that most pergolas are large, this compact version serves as an accent to a cedar deck. It serves as a boundary marker rather than a shelter.

MAKING THE CONNECTION: TIPS FOR PAIRING A PERGOLA AND A DECK

- The connection starts with the posts; always try to attach them to the existing deck frame. For new structures simply substitute them for shorter versions that would have served as railing posts. Using longer posts will provide the height the pergola needs.
- For pergola posts that aren't located directly above the deck footings, you may have to dig and pour additional concrete footings under the deck. If the deck floor height is too low to allow that, remove some of the planking to provide access to the subframe of beams and joists. Then

reinforce that framework and attach the pergola posts with large bolts and refit the deck planking as required.
- Accessory assemblies on the deck (railings, built-in benches, and so on) are ideal attachment points for a pergola, as long as they aren't its principal supports.
- Aim for three key connection points for the posts: to footings or framing beneath the deck floor, to a point at midheight such as a railing, and to the pergola "roof" assembly at the upper end. This arrangement provides the greatest strength and stability.

Building Pergolas With Decks

Even if your existing deck doesn't need replacing or rebuilding, adding a pergola is often a good opportunity for a cosmetic upgrade. Deck railings especially are good candidates for customization. They are often generic designs aimed at code compliance and low-cost installation, and many look like an afterthought because they don't match the detailing on the house.

Given a deck frame that's structurally sound and planking that's in good shape, look first to the perimeter railing posts as a starting point for adding a pergola. If they are solidly attached to footings and project upward through the deck frame, they offer an ideal anchor. They are likely made from 4×4 stock and will extend to about 36 inches above the deck floor. Pergolas often use 6×6 posts, and for retrofit designs you can use a hollow box post (made from 1-inch-thick lumber) rather than a solid timber. A box post can fit like a sleeve over the existing railing post and extend to the height required for the pergola. If you want to keep your railing design as is, modify only the posts required to frame the pergola, then shorten the affected railing sections slightly to fit. For an even stronger architectural effect, consider building column enclosures or pedestals around the lower portions of the pergola posts. This will give you room to repeat trim or siding details from the house for a custom look.

As with almost any other type of garden structure, pergolas can vary from the basic theme. This deck has a pair of narrow bookend pergolas (one covered in foliage, at left) rather than a single structure that covers the entire area. Despite the open ceiling, the added height still gives the deck a greater sense of enclosure.

Simply extending railing posts upward creates the opportunity for retrofitting a pergola onto this deck. These railing columns were built outward and covered with wood shingles to match the house siding.

Attaching a pergola frame to the house along two adjacent sides means the outboard post connections can be simpler, because they don't have to withstand heavy lateral (sideways) loads. They do, however, transfer the weight of the overhead frame onto the deck, so they should be positioned directly above footings or beams.

Wall-Mounted Pergolas Above Doorways

A shallow wall-mounted pergola that graces a wide door or window opening reflects the true "projecting roof" pedigree of this type of structure. Like a front porch or a deck, it also creates a distinct transition that softens the break between exterior and interior spaces.

The pergola shown on the opposite page features the simplest of construction techniques. Two matching assemblies of horizontal girders (basically short projecting beams) and diagonal knee braces support a pair of long crossbeams, which are topped by a series of short 2×2 purlins, creating the appearance of a horizontal ladder. The purlins provide support for a climbing plant but could easily stay unadorned, especially if the pergola were painted or stained in an accent or contrasting color distinct from the siding and trim.

Proper mounting and support are critical to this project.

The two end assemblies feature stout timber screws that lock the components together and also secure them firmly to the wall by means of a vertical 2×2 cleat. It's essential that the mounting screws attach to the wall framing itself and not to the surface trim or siding. Because of its light weight and good weather resistance, western red cedar is a good choice for this type of pergola. A pair of 2×4 crossbeams can safely span 8 feet, but check your local building codes. Wider spans will require increasing the crossbeam size to 2×6 or 2×8 lumber.

This over-the-door pergola reflects the more formal design of the brick home, featuring elaborate curved braces, scrollwork on the beams and joists, and a subtle two-tone color scheme. The substantial heft of the end brackets and crossbeam ensures plenty of strength to support the upper assembly and also makes a bold architectural statement appropriate for the scale of the home.

You could hardly find a more user-friendly project to tackle than this garage door pergola. Compact and simple, it's an affordable one-weekend project and an easy way to dress up a garage.

CONSTRUCTING A PERGOLA OVER A DOOR OR WINDOW

1. 2×4 crossbeams (2 pieces)
(Max span 8'; use 2×6 up to 12' span)

2. 2×2 mounting cleat (2 pieces)

3. 2×6 fascia/trim

4. Siding

5. 2×4 knee braces (4 pieces)

6. 2×6 girders with scroll-cut ends
(4 pieces)

7. 2×2 rungs

Note: All lumber is western red cedar.

Freestanding Pergolas

The many virtues of attached pergolas can't overcome one potentially fundamental drawback: What if you want yours somewhere else?

Opting for a structure separate from the house involves a few minor engineering upgrades, but you have the advantage of choosing the ideal site for enjoying the landscape rather than being limited by tethering it to the house.

Aside from placement options a lone garden structure offers another kind of freedom—more elbow room for the design. Being farther from the house means being able to tailor the pergola more to its garden setting, or going eclectic and not worrying about what matches the window shutters. Color, materials, accessories—all of these elements can depart more from the home's established style and still leave you with a structure suited to its surroundings. And like a seating arbor tucked away in a quiet corner of the yard, a pergola placed in a remote location feels like a restful retreat, so if it's a personal sanctuary you're after, let yourself go free.

Close proximity to the building on the left would have made this pergola easy to attach, but standing alone and symmetrical it has more visual importance.

Even pergolas that don't extend overhead can create a convincing sense of enclosure, proving the design axiom that sometimes less is more.

DESIGNING AND SITING A FREESTANDING PERGOLA

- Look for a spot that's a natural focal point in the yard or garden, or one adjacent to other landscape features you want to enjoy.
- You won't have the house to block views, so choose a location that doesn't completely eliminate your privacy; if you feel as if you're on display for the neighbors, you'll have a hard time relaxing.
- Limit the height to around 8 feet unless there are large trees or buildings close by; a tall structure in an otherwise empty yard can seem misplaced.
- For the most stable structure, embed the posts in concrete footings that extend below the frost line. If that's not possible, bolt them to the top of the footings using heavy bracket hardware and use knee braces at the top of the structure.
- Consider a narrow, perimeter pergola around the outside of a sitting area rather than a wide structure that covers the area; it's less costly to build but creates a similar effect in defining the space.

Though they may sacrifice some convenience, freestanding pergolas are often better than attached structures for creating a perfect getaway spot in the yard. This simple version helps create an intimate seating group.

Pergolas With Fences and Trellises

Although pergolas typically are substantial structures big enough to stand on their own literally and visually, their open-frame nature tends to leave them a little short on privacy. For a greater sense of seclusion, team a pergola with a trellis or fence.

Often just one or two sides of a pergola need view control; if you want to screen more than that, instead consider building a gazebo, screen house, or other structure with partial walls or privacy panels. Pergolas are meant to be open structures, so your aim should be to control and direct the incoming and outgoing views, not to eliminate them entirely.

As with any building project, your plan should include any accessory structures from the start. Incorporating them later might not be difficult or add any significant structural requirements, but thinking ahead can result in a more professional and deliberate design. For example you might design a 15-foot-long pergola with posts spaced every 5 feet, creating three open bays, then decide later to add prefabricated lattice panels on one side for a trellis. You shop for the trellis panels only to discover they are all 4 feet wide, requiring a splice and extra support framing in the wider bays. The building process would be simpler and the look cleaner if you planned a 16-foot pergola and added another post, creating 4-foot bays that could each be covered with a single trellis panel.

This grouping offers a great example of how garden structures work well as an ensemble. The arbor announces the entrance to the patio, the flanking pergolas establish seating and dining areas, and the matching fence helps enclose the area and create a little privacy.

With a stone wall behind and a pergola roof above, this dining alcove provides privacy and protection. The infill trellis panel atop the wall is a critical feature in the design. Without it the gap would create an odd feeling of exposure in an otherwise sheltered environment.

With its dark finish offering dramatic contrast to the surrounding greenery, this hybrid structure combines a tunnel arbor and a pergola. Trellis panels surround a small brick patio offset from the flagstone path, creating a cozy seating alcove.

Tucked amid a well-manicured formal garden, this triangular pergola is a striking focal point—small but nicely detailed with a classic white painted finish. The swinging bench makes it all the more inviting and versatile.

Corner Pergolas

Just as large square or rectangular pergolas can mimic the effect of an enclosed room despite their wide-open design, smaller partial versions can help define outdoor spaces even when they don't actually cover them. These structures serve as outposts or perimeter markers, creating a recognizable boundary where the space begins and ends, and they are especially effective at corners.

Whether L-shape or triangular, a corner pergola is a useful option in smaller gardens or in areas where you want to define the borders without creating an actual enclosure. They are a simple and indirect sort of shelter, one with a presence and effect you notice without it being front and center. They highlight a focused area that in most cases is already inherently comfortable, creating quiet seating areas or conversation nooks where people naturally want to be. Think about your favorite restaurant table—is it in the middle of a large and busy room or tucked away in a nice private corner with views you can enjoy on your own terms?

If entertaining on a large patio or deck is more your style, a full-size pergola is probably a better choice. But for a little voluntary seclusion, it's hard to beat these inviting and more personal structures. If you still need persuading, you can take additional comfort in their practical advantages of being easier and less costly to build.

Although it occupies a flagstone patio with a square outline, this pergola was deliberately designed as a corner structure. The clipped front corner creates a wide diagonal entry that offers access to both the adjacent house and a terraced landscape nearby.

Pergolas With Curved Tops

Like smaller garden structures, pergolas can take on much more personality and character when some of their straight lines and angular geometry give way to arches and other curved architectural elements. On pergolas these features are in principle the same as you would find on arbors or trellises, but the larger scale does introduce some complexity.

First the longer spans in pergolas mean that overhead beams have more structural work to do, and compromises in strength that might be acceptable in smaller components can be dangerous in larger structures. For example solid wood is stronger in its long-grain direction than it is across the grain, and cutting a curved shape from a wide board tends to concentrate stresses in that weaker area.

To avoid problems, curves cut in solid stock should be shallow to ensure that plenty of the stronger long-grain area of the board remains intact. A good rule is to never remove more than one-third of the original width anywhere along the board.

Second using stack or bentwood lamination techniques (see pages 118–120) is much harder to do with a 12-foot pergola beam than it is with a 4-foot-wide arch for an arbor and requires more and stronger clamps, larger bending

Shallow curves on a pergola roof normally can be cut from wide stock, especially when multiple boards are sandwiched together to make thicker beams. If in doubt run the design details by local building officials or a professional engineer before proceeding.

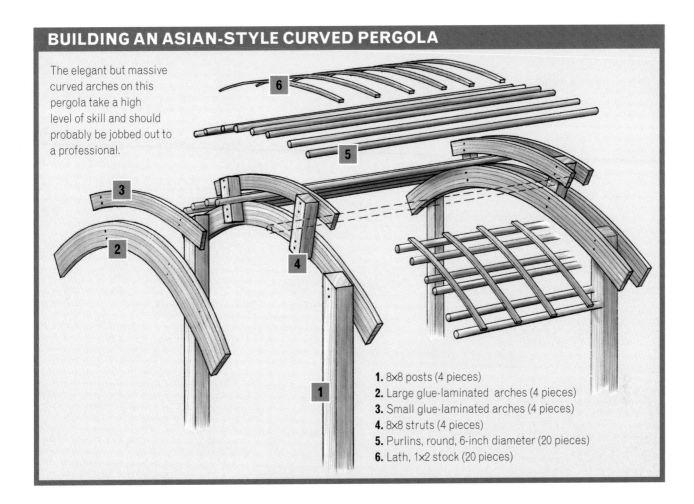

BUILDING AN ASIAN-STYLE CURVED PERGOLA

The elegant but massive curved arches on this pergola take a high level of skill and should probably be jobbed out to a professional.

1. 8×8 posts (4 pieces)
2. Large glue-laminated arches (4 pieces)
3. Small glue-laminated arches (4 pieces)
4. 8×8 struts (4 pieces)
5. Purlins, round, 6-inch diameter (20 pieces)
6. Lath, 1×2 stock (20 pieces)

jigs, and bigger machines to mill the stock and the finished lamination. This doesn't rule out arches and curves, but it does mean you should hire this work out to a professional millwork contractor or a shop that specializes in glue-laminated beams.

That said the added expense for this feature opens up a lot of design options that can make a pergola unique and striking. It's especially useful in giving more architectural presence to freestanding structures.

A fusion of Asian and contemporary styles, this freestanding pergola has clean lines and spare detailing that make it look simple. The two-tiered roof, however, requires highly skilled professional expertise to produce the large curved laminated beams.

When attached to the house, a dining pergola like this can more easily be fitted with amenities such as wiring for a ceiling fan. This patio is big enough for more than one dining group, so the pergola is similarly expansive.

 # Pergolas for Dining

Pergolas are a natural venue for outdoor dining. Most full-size versions offer a comfortable gathering place, room for a table and chairs, and—if attached to the house—convenient access for carrying food and dishes to and from the kitchen.

Given the right weather most people enjoy occasional meals outdoors. The experience is usually informal, shared with friends or family, and seems more removed from daily cares than ordinary meals in the house. Alfresco dining is inherently relaxing; you might associate it with a picnic or a vacation—even an unforgettable dinner at a Parisian sidewalk cafe. A pergola can't take you to Europe, but it can let an otherwise ordinary backyard become the setting for memorable meals. A tranquil garden setting only sweetens the deal.

Positioned poolside and with sunlight filtering through its vine-clad roof arches, this pergola is a comfortable dining venue even on the hottest summer day. The metal in the overhead structure has a lighter look than wood and is echoed in the wrought-iron dining set.

DINING PERGOLA TIPS

- Make it at least 10 feet across in each direction to accommodate a dining table and chairs comfortably.
- Equip it with a firm and reasonably flat floor. It doesn't have to be a concrete slab, but rough flagstone or gravel makes it difficult for diners to move their chairs.
- Place it close enough to the house to provide reasonable convenience.
- Provide shelter—buildings or windbreaks—if the site is regularly subject to strong breezes or gusts.
- Wire it for electricity so you can install a ceiling fan or overhead light fixture (controlled with a dimmer switch). You may prefer dining by candlelight or starlight, but having light for cleanup afterward is really handy. And on muggy afternoons a ceiling fan is a godsend.
- Cover it with small-grid lattice if you want shade or if you're patient and plant a large perennial vine, in two or three years you'll have a good canopy of foliage.

Pergolas With Outdoor Kitchens

The role of a pergola as a garden structure, a pedigree that goes back centuries, is being augmented by a relative newcomer to the American backyard: the built-in outdoor kitchen.

The growing popularity of outdoor kitchens, whether as simple grilling stations or as well-equipped culinary centers for preparing and cleaning up entire meals, has given the pergola another part to play in outdoor design.

When combining outdoor kitchens with possibly combustible building components, such as wood, some common-sense rules apply.

Place the pergola's wood components a safe distance from grills, smokers, gas burners, and any other sources of combustion. Typically these appliances are installed in brick or stone surrounds so there's no fire danger, and these masonry bases can serve as platforms for installing posts or other structural parts of the pergola. (A fire extinguisher stored onsite is a worthwhile precaution nonetheless.)

Because the pergola's open top doesn't provide any real protection from the elements, all of the kitchen amenities and components should be designed to withstand exposure to rain, harsh sunlight, and—in wintry climates—snow and ice. Stainless-steel cabinetry and undercounter appliances are readily available for this application, and they are worth the extra expense.(If a rain-proof shelter is essential, consider a more pavilionlike design. Turn to Chapter 6 for examples.)

A pergola adds stature and focus to an outdoor kitchen and helps tie it aesthetically to the house or other landscape features, and that's often enough reason to pair the two.

This pergola unfies what could otherwise be a patchwork arrangement of dining area, entries, and an outdoor cooking area. The roof over part of it is a nice touch and provides rainproofing in the most important areas.

This pergola merely borrows some counterspace from the outdoor kitchen. Separate pedestals would have served the same purpose, but this approach ties the package together nicely and doesn't compromise the kitchen's safety or function.

Rustic Pergolas

Like rustic arbors and other smaller structures, pergolas built in a similar style can feature a variety of materials, from rough-hewn timbers or rusted iron columns to twisted branches used in their natural form. The environment is often similar too, perhaps a simple country setting with an old milk can serving as a chair or a wooded area with an Old West frontier look.

Where pergolas differ is their larger scale and the extra care required to ensure their structural integrity. Ordinary fasteners or techniques that might secure the lightweight branches of a trellis or an arbor are often inadequate for heavier structures or larger spans. Deck screws that would easily hold a rustic lattice panel together can snap without warning if asked to bear the stresses of a large timber joint; bolts or timber screws—sized and heat treated for such applications—are required for these harsher circumstances. With some branches weighing more than 100 pounds, the consequences of a failure are plenty serious.

Another factor, at least with live-branch construction, is that you can't rely on consistent strength from one branch to the next. A bark-covered post or beam can have hidden internal defects that reveal themselves only through a structural failure. Even if the branch starts out sound, it can degrade over time without giving any indication you can see. And if you're plucking raw material out of a local woodlot or from miscellaneous urban trees, you may get random species with widely differing properties.

In contrast milled lumber is graded by both species and quality, and there's lots of engineering data—not to mention code requirements—in support of using certain sizes and grades of lumber in a given situation. This means that when designing a rustic pergola, you need to err on the side of caution and use larger posts and beams to provide an adequate margin of safety, and it sometimes takes more than an educated guess. Check to see if local building codes might require an independent engineering appraisal of a rustic structure.

Rustic structures allow you to mix and match elements without regard for precise style statements. This pergola is an eclectic blend of live-branch framework and picket fence sidewalls sheltering vintage metal patio furniture.

Building rustic structures doesn't necessarily mean abandoning all the principles of formal construction. This pergola features the same mix of posts, beams, knee braces, girders, and purlins that would be common for a structure made of dimensioned lumber. The bulkier look comes from using slightly oversize stock common with this style.

5 Gazebos

Few other garden structures have claimed such diverse roles in both public and private settings. Gazebos are a quintessential element in village greens, serving as bandstands, community icons, and platforms for political oratory.

There's something wonderfully old-fashioned about the idea of a gazebo. You may envision a fanciful summer spot where a Victorian lady or gentleman would easily be at home—though some gazebos are sleek, contemporary affairs. Whatever the style of the gazebo, all have an unmistakable look and presence.

In your own garden a gazebo can provide a setting for group events that range from a casual picnic to a formal wedding but just as easily lend itself to a solitary afternoon break or a lazy hour spent watching the sun go down. And it's nice to look at when you're not in it. What other structure could beat that versatility?

About Gazebos

The first gazebos were most likely sheltered viewing platforms built for function, not form. Their purpose was to let the owner view the countryside from all directions, keep an eye on holdings, and determine if enemies were approaching.

Gazebos are also probably related to observation towers and huge lanterns that once were part of castles and large estates. Those architectural elements were frequently round or octagonal, had half-height walls that allowed clear views of the surrounding countryside, and were often topped with an ornate roof.

The simpler viewing platforms were often perched atop tall structures, but pluck them off and set them directly on the ground and you have what today is universally recognized as a gazebo.

Building circular towers and platforms made sense back then because workers laid individual stones. Today when wood and metal make up gazebo walls, especially if they're going to be fitted with windows or screen panels, a geometric faceted form such as an octagon is easier to execute.

Gazebos can have 6, 8, 10, or even 12 sides, but in their classic form they still allow 360-degree views. The original design may have included that to sight hostile visitors early, but today you can appreciate the panoramic view afforded by a gazebo to take in surrounding beauty, whether it is a seashore, a mountain range, or simply a pleasant backyard.

ANATOMY OF A GAZEBO

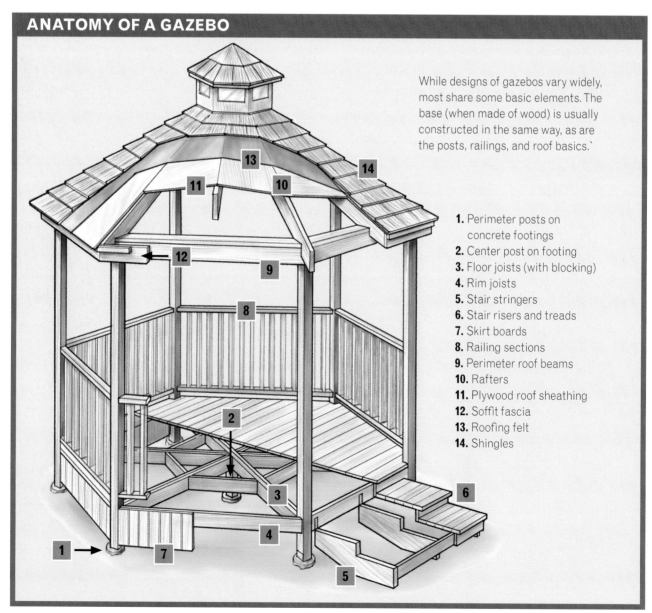

While designs of gazebos vary widely, most share some basic elements. The base (when made of wood) is usually constructed in the same way, as are the posts, railings, and roof basics.`

1. Perimeter posts on concrete footings
2. Center post on footing
3. Floor joists (with blocking)
4. Rim joists
5. Stair stringers
6. Stair risers and treads
7. Skirt boards
8. Railing sections
9. Perimeter roof beams
10. Rafters
11. Plywood roof sheathing
12. Soffit fascia
13. Roofing felt
14. Shingles

This is certainly an idyllic setting for a gazebo—but almost any landscape, however humble, can benefit from this classic structure. The open framework, decorative trim, and small cupola are signature elements that define gazebos and make them instantly recognizable.

WHAT MAKES A GREAT GAZEBO?

- Ideally a gazebo should be positioned for the best possible outward views and be slightly elevated.
- If you'll want to be able to dine with friends and family, make sure there's plenty of room for a table for four, six, or eight—or more. And remember that a space of 3 to 4 feet on all sides of the table is needed to accommodate chairs and people getting in and out of them.
- If lounging is your goal, measure the type and number of furniture pieces you want. Then allow at least 2 feet between each piece to allow for people walking around.
- As gazebos became less utilitarian and more recreational, ornament and finish became the hallmarks of a well-crafted structure. It doesn't have to be gingerbread Victorian, but make sure yours features at least a few design flourishes through the use of trim and color.
- Cedar and redwood have long been perennial favorites for use in gazebos. Whatever the wood species (or metal type), the material quality should be high, especially since there typically is little or no sheathing or siding to hide the structural framework.
- The roof is often the only solid feature of a gazebo, and it's usually the most prominent. The contour, materials, and detail work deserve a lot of attention, much more than you'd normally give another structure such as a shed.

This charming structure blends the classic gazebo shape with features that suggest a centuries-old English conservatory. The additional protection afforded by French doors and windows allows the gazebo to be furnished much as an interior space would be.

About Gazebos

Siting a gazebo is everything. Because they are large, placing one badly in a landscape will be painfully apparent.

One helpful hint in siting a gazebo is to look at other elements in the landscape and see how they relate to each other. A gazebo might look strange plunked into the middle of an expanse of green lawn—but it might take on the lure of a destination, a place to get away from it all, placed at the far end of a lawn.

Gazebos also are effective when they are situated to take in views, for example, on the top of slopes or hills. They're also perfect for siting along a river, creek, or other water view. If you're considering installing a large water feature or maybe already have one, a gazebo alongside it will look very logical.

Since gazebos are like stages, with their inhabitants on display, it's important to feel comfortable sitting wherever the gazebo is located. Thus placing a gazebo along a street, a busy alley, or the neighbor's property line can be problematic.

However if you must put a gazebo where privacy is going to be an issue, you can remedy the problem somewhat with good design: Incorporate lattice or trelliswork on the sides of the gazebo exposed to public view.

The design of the roof is important. In very temperate, cool, dry climates you may be able to get away with openwork or lath. However in other climates part of a gazebo's appeal is that it protects those enjoying it from rain and sun and if you can easily run electricity to your gazebo, consider installing a ceiling fan, which can make the space feel 10°F/12°C cooler.

Electricity in a gazebo has another advantage: It allows you to light the space, making it easier to enjoy after-sundown meals without fumbling and stumbling.

Perched overhead almost like a giant mushroom cap, the gazebo's rustic shingle roof creates a kind of fairy tale simplicity in the garden. This setting demonstrates that although gazebos are often built for views, they can also serve as quiet garden sanctuaries.

Gazebos From Kits

Designing and building a gazebo from scratch can be quite a feat. Their geometry makes them significantly more complex than the average garden structure. That can translate into higher costs for custom professionally built versions, or some intimidating math for do-it-yourselfers who might otherwise be confident when it comes to their amateur carpentry skills.

However their design complexity has spawned a vigorous market for kits that can make a gazebo achievable for the ambitious amateur and greatly speed the process (and thereby reduce labor costs) for professional builders. It's a user friendly and affordable way to add a gazebo to your yard or garden.

The vast majority of gazebos these days are built from kits—and with good reason. With a kit the design work is already complete, so you can concentrate on just the foundation and assembly work. The complicated calculations and precise measuring are done for you, although grading the site and positioning concrete pier footings still require careful work. Building instructions

WHAT'S IN A GAZEBO KIT

Do Expect:
- Precut parts made of clear and/or select grades of cedar or redwood lumber.
- Some preassembled sections, typically including deck segments and railing sections.
- All the nails, screws, and other hardware required for assembly.
- A comprehensive illustrated instruction manual or video.
- Access to a toll-free help line.
- Cost savings because the design and much of the labor are already accomplished.

Don't Expect:
- The foundation; your structure will typically require a slab floor or separate concrete pier footings to support the gazebo deck structure.
- Automatic approval for building permits; code compliance is still a matter for local building officials, who may require an engineer's approval for your gazebo kit.
- Elaborate joinery or detailing; keep in mind that these structures, while not necessarily mass produced, are designed for efficient manufacturing processes. That means connections are usually simple butt or lap joints secured with fasteners. If you want dovetail or mortise-and-tenon craftsmanship, go custom and expect to pay accordingly.

are fairly clear and may even include an instructional video, and some companies provide a toll-free help line you can call for technical help. Just as important, all the parts or sections are precut or preassembled, saving you a lot of time setting up tools or assembly jigs.

Finally the requisite materials are all provided, with the exception of the finish roofing materials such as flashing, roofing felt (asphalt-impregnated paper), and shingles. This means you'll have everything from the right lumber types and grades to all the necessary fasteners and hardware, sparing you or your contractor time (and probably confusion) during the building process.

Prefinished kits offered by many manufacturers are especially convenient. Ideally the components will have a factory-applied finish that includes a primer/sealer plus a durable top coat. The wood floor sections should be supported by concrete pier footings, which can be covered with mulch or a groundcover.

Even for a relatively simple gazebo design such as this, the geometry for the posts, railings, and roof sections can get tricky. A kit eliminates logistical and design headaches yet also allows some degree of customization—in this case creating a base that accommodates an eccentrically tilting tree.

Gazebos as Part of Decks and Porches

Gazebos are typically built as freestanding structures, but like arbors and pergolas they can be attached to a home or another landscape feature such as a deck. The combination often enhances the looks and function of both structures, but the same rule applies as before: The closer or more directly attached a garden structure is to the house, the more it should share design elements such as color scheme, materials, or trim details.

For example pairing a gazebo with a deck should involve extending the deck planking into the gazebo, although the pattern or orientation will likely change to reflect the shape of the gazebo. Also you should continue the deck railing with identical sections for the gazebo walls. Using two different railing styles will look odd and make the combination read visually as two small and mismatched structures rather than a larger integrated one.

Tying a gazebo directly to the house introduces a few more elements to consider, especially roofing materials and exterior millwork. The roofing should be an exact match, but the trim might allow some leeway. Stay sympathetic with the style and don't introduce jarring contrasts such as pairing a stark modernist treatment with a colorful Victorian or a rustic cottage look. However you can usually get away with a slightly more ornate treatment on the gazebo, just enough to suggest that it's as much about fun as function.

Shared materials and colors ensure that this gazebo and deck are a well-integrated pair. The river rock foundation and simple baluster railing are the clearest visual cues, and the white lath roof gives the gazebo an airy look appropriate for the setting.

The traditional flavor of a gazebo can sometimes disguise a very modern feature, such as a deck-mounted hot tub. The gazebo protects the tub and its occupants, and it also makes the tub more inconspicuous even when viewed from the deck itself.

Because of their odd shape, gazebos attached directly to homes often need a transition to make the connection work. In this case a small porch extension does the trick. The scrollwork trim echoes just a few elements on the house instead of being an exact style match.

Finished with a semitransparent latex stain and surrounded by mature plants, this gazebo yields no clue that it was built from a kit rather than from scratch. The double cupola would have been much tougher to build without the prefabricated components.

Gazebo Construction

Whether your gazebo is from a kit or custom made, you need a properly prepared site and a foundation to support the structure. Some versions sit on a concrete slab, but more common is a wood deck floor that rests on individual pier footings arranged in a circle, with one center pier for internal support. This project features these individual footings.

Try to choose a fairly level area and one that highlights the gazebo's role as a viewing platform. The kit's instruction manual will provide information on the number and spacing of the pier footings, which can be indicated with wood stakes driven into the ground. Use a string tied to the center stake to score a circular outline in the soil, then drive the first pair of stakes, one opposite the other. Depending on the number of panels or sides (this version has 10), follow the layout instructions to place the stakes for the remaining footings. Dig the holes, then fit cardboard tube forms in place and level them.

The pier footings are identical to those discussed in previous chapters and require similar preparation and depth to prevent cracking and/or frost heave. Let the concrete cure for several days before erecting the structure. Keep in mind that the kit you buy may differ from the example shown; these steps illustrate the most common stages of construction.

Even though designs of gazebos can vary widely, there are still some basic steps to follow. This gazebo's base has been constructed and now it's time to erect the sides.

While every gazebo is different, there are some basic assembly steps that most share.

1. This gazebo uses a prefabricated wood hub. It serves as the center connection for the gazebo's floor joists, which radiate toward the perimeter like spokes in a wheel. All of these components were precut and ready to install.

2. When all the floor joists are fitted, their outboard ends should each rest on a concrete pier, with at least 2 inches of the board supported. Other framing components will be attached at these ends, so there should be plenty of footing surface left for support.

3. Fastening the rim joist segments around the perimeter of the gazebo will help establish the proper alignment and spacing of the joists. Once you've done that, use cedar shims to adjust each corner until the entire floor assembly is level.

4. Because exact alignment of the pier footings is difficult, you have to drill for anchor bolts after the floor frame is built rather than embed them in the wet concrete when it's poured. Use a hammer drill to bore for an expansion-type anchor bolt, and use that to secure a mounting bracket for the joist (inset).

5. Temporarily place a few of the flooring deck sections so you can align the center blocks and screw them in place. Then fit the remaining sections, adjust them for uniform spacing, and attach them to the floor joists with screws.

6. Arrange the prefabricated wall/railing frames (inset photo) around the floor assembly, then connect them to each other and to the decking. For this step recruit a helper who can hold the frames steady while you work.

7. At this stage the basic structural frame of the gazebo is complete. Top plates are added to reinforce the connections between the wall frames, and the roof rafters and center block installed.

8. Careful work during the initial assembly stages pays off as you get the precut roof sheathing panels in place. Tack each panel in place with two partially driven nails until all of the sections are fitted and aligned, then finish nailing them securely.

9. Roof fascia creates a more finished look and provides additional support for the frame and roofing panels. As with the roof sheathing, tack these temporarily in place until all are fitted properly, then nail them securely.

10. After installing drip-edge flashing and stapling a layer of roofing felt in place, shingle the main roof one section at a time. Trim the shingles where the sections abut one another, then cover the seams with rows of ridge shingles. Add any cupolas over the shingles on the main roof.

Gazebo Roofs

With such an interesting footprint to follow, the roof of a gazebo offers the opportunity for variations that can give the structure personality or establish a definitive architectural presence or style. It can turn the gazebo into something exceptional.

If this seems an ambitious claim to make for a single feature, consider how many iconic buildings owe their status to a distinctive roofline—the Chrysler building in New York, the Sydney Opera House, or any number of historic cathedrals, mosques, and temples worldwide. These buildings feature roof structures that identify them, define them, and set the tone for the way they are regarded by their communities. Even if you don't want to get that ambitious

With a tiered roof and vented cupola teamed with lattice screens and a simple baluster railing, this gazebo captures the quintessential nature and traditional charm these structures offer. The open vents under each roof help promote air circulation to keep the seating area below cooler.

The style or impact of a gazebo's roof isn't limited to merely its top layer. This simple but classic structure supports a crisp copper roof on a series of framed openings and arched panels that work their way around the structure. This detailing contributes a lot to the formal personality.

with a gazebo in your own garden, it helps to consider the statement your gazebo's roof will make.

If standard kits don't seem to have the roof options you'd like, don't hesitate to ask the manufacturer about other choices. Some will adapt the roof assembly from another kit in their line and let you order it separately. If they don't have exactly what you want, see if they offer custom design and fabrication services just for the roof. Even when adding that to a standard kit, you'd still spend less than you would for an entire custom gazebo.

Set back in a distant corner of the yard, this inviting retreat will put any day's stresses in perspective. The turned ornamental posts help echo the charming bell-shape roof, which softens the normally angular geometry of these structures.

This bell-shape gazebo roof benefits from a delicate and airy look that would be impossible to achieve with a dark or solid roof. The narrow lath strips conform easily to the curved rafters, making the construction simpler than it looks.

Suggestive of an astronomical observatory or an alien spacecraft, this dome-style gazebo roof combines with grid columns and roof extensions to create the flavor of a traditional English conservatory. This kind of metalwork typically calls for custom fabrication by highly skilled craftsmen.

Gazebo Roofs

Even with the relatively straightforward geometry on simple gazebo roofs, cutting and fitting rafters and roof sheathing for these structures can be a bit complicated. That's part of the reason many do-it-yourselfers opt for kits. It's also why some contractors and manufacturers specialize in designing and building gazebos: It allows them to standardize models and not have to calculate new specifications for each project.

The roof complexity may well be a key factor in deciding whether you want to build a gazebo yourself or hire it out, and if the latter, whom to pick as a designer/builder. The simplest roofs are single-tiered versions with uniform flat triangular sections that meet at the peak. This keeps the rafter layout and cutting simpler and the shingling easier. But many gazebos are more intricate: Some will have two or more roof tiers, and others a small cupola vent. Many

are bell shape or domed, often with a slight flair around the perimeter to help divert rainfall from the structure. Make the decision about roof type and shape early in the planning stage while you're thinking about site placement, paint colors, and other features.

And whether you construct the gazebo yourself or hire a contractor, the best tactic usually is to build and shingle the roof separately and then have a crew hoist it atop the wall frames. The work gets done faster and more safely if it's completed on the ground rather than while you or the contractor are perched on a small steep roof.

This example of a lath roof shows how an open, airy roof increases ventilation and creates dramatic patterns of light and shadow below. Warm arid climates are ideal for this type of roof.

Rustic Gazebos

The rustic look popular for arbors and pergolas translates also to gazebos, and often for the same reasons. Country settings, farmhouses, and vacation retreats can be the perfect backdrop for a garden structure that's casual and downright earthy.

As with other rustic outdoor structures, a gazebo of the same style can feature a mix of materials and motifs. The live-branch technique so popular for trellises and other small structures confronts its limitations here as it does with pergolas. It's not that it can't be done, but the longer spans and greater structural requirements mean that the casual construction techniques of nailed or twine-tied joints will not suffice. And it may be hard to find a contractor accustomed to building this way; if so search out local artisans who can engineer and experiment with odd materials.

Rustic design doesn't limit you to sifting through piles of twisted tree branches and fashioning crude work with a dull hatchet. You can use rough sawn or hand-hewn timbers, rusted metal parts from old cars or tractors, vintage or eclectic items—anything that suggests simple handwork or lacks polish. Got old wagon wheel spokes, mismatched porch posts, and floorboards from salvaged chicken coops? Those will do nicely. Above all try to have fun with rustic design. It's meant to showcase a simpler way of seeing the world, and it's a reminder that with time everyone acquires character by getting a little rough around the edges.

Rustic doesn't always have to mean all-natural. The pillars on this rustic gazebo are wood gleaned from a beach, but the roof is a salvaged 10-foot satellite dish. Originally planted with nasturtiums, the dish's shallow rim now hosts a variety of wild plants. Underneath, weathered logs have been sliced into stumps to form the gazebo's sides.

This live-branch gazebo illustrates a good principle for this type of rustic construction. Use fairly uniform components (straight poles, for example) for the structural frame and let the fill material be more freeform in order to add interest and character. Inspect these structures regularly to ensure they are still sound; the irregular surfaces and bark can hide decay and stress cracks that might signal the need to replace structural parts.

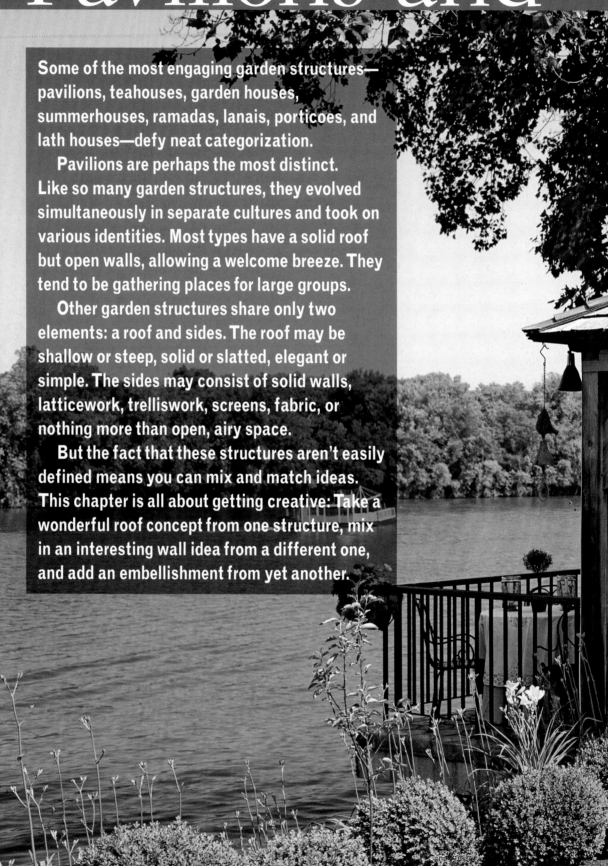

6 Pavilions and

Some of the most engaging garden structures—pavilions, teahouses, garden houses, summerhouses, ramadas, lanais, porticoes, and lath houses—defy neat categorization.

Pavilions are perhaps the most distinct. Like so many garden structures, they evolved simultaneously in separate cultures and took on various identities. Most types have a solid roof but open walls, allowing a welcome breeze. They tend to be gathering places for large groups.

Other garden structures share only two elements: a roof and sides. The roof may be shallow or steep, solid or slatted, elegant or simple. The sides may consist of solid walls, latticework, trelliswork, screens, fabric, or nothing more than open, airy space.

But the fact that these structures aren't easily defined means you can mix and match ideas. This chapter is all about getting creative: Take a wonderful roof concept from one structure, mix in an interesting wall idea from a different one, and add an embellishment from yet another.

Other Structures

About Pavilions

The most ancient pavilions were as basic as you can get—a few upright poles stuck in the ground, with a fabric or animal-skin cover stretched overhead. They provided shade on sunny days and some protection from the rain but remained open on the sides for ventilation and probably for the sake of simplicity; they could be erected and broken down quickly, making them ideal for nomadic cultures. Today these portable versions are called tents or canopies and the word "pavilion" is reserved for permanent structures that perform a similar function.

Pavilions have obviously come a long way and today the word evokes elegance and a sense of occasion. In public places there are dancing pavilions, food pavilions, band pavilions, tea pavilions, and pavilions used as places to pause and view beautiful water views—whether the view is an ocean, lake, river, or backyard water feature.

It's not surprising that modern shade-providing leisure structures like pavilions are popular in areas where people like to sit and soak up solar rays. Pavilions can go anywhere, but sunny poolside and waterfront locations seem to be their natural habitat. The structure helps give definition to the setting and provides a welcome retreat when the midday heat gets to be too much to handle. With the relief of shade and refreshing breezes through the open sides, it's not uncommon to see temperature differences of 10°F/12°C underneath a pavilion's roof. When summer peaks, this is no small matter.

Pavilions also tend to be larger than some other garden structures—10 or 12 feet across in either direction is a minimum, and that's considered small. Grand scale often translates into higher construction and materials costs, but the result is an upscale look that says if you're going to indulge in a beautiful landscape structure, do it right.

With its graceful reflection fluttering in the water, this pavilion creates a luxurious backdrop for the pool. The layered grid roof and latticework support columns give the structure a light and graceful look, while the scale is still large enough to house a dining table and chairs.

Closed or solid roofs are the rule for pavilions, but like gazebos these structures sometimes sport vented or lath roofs such as this one. Fluted columns lend a classical touch, and a privacy trellis screens the view to and from a neighboring yard.

Fit for a Roman emperor, this Mediterranean-style pavilion rests on stout columns and features a quality touch—red clay roof tiles that match the terra-cotta pool surround. Unlike a gazebo perched for viewing, pavilions like this tend to nestle into the landscape.

Dramatic settings for pavilions don't always involve formal gardens or mansions. This pondside structure appears to float. Full-width curtains, shown tied at the corner posts, can be extended for privacy or protection against the weather.

About Pavilions

Some garden areas or backyard settings may be ideal for a simple structure such as an arbor or pergola, so if you're thinking about a pavilion consider whether its upgrades are features you actually want. The closed-roof option has practical value, fending off rain and the harshest sun at midday, and it usually represents the biggest design difference. But you should plan to build bigger for a pavilion, and with better materials. When the footprint is too tiny or the goods cheap, the pavilion can look more like a bus stop enclosure than a garden structure.

Also the setting should be appropriate. You don't need a windswept oceanfront estate or an acre-size backyard with a million-dollar swimming pool, but if your garden area is very small or simple, a pavilion (unless it's quite small and perhaps made of rustic materials) might seem like an odd grandiose gesture, one that seems out of place or that makes the modest surroundings seem inadequate. It might turn out to be the architectural equivalent of wearing pearls to a potluck picnic. Worse still it might detract from an otherwise charming garden if it overpowers rather than enhances the space. So let your garden be your guide. If it has the square footage and style, a pavilion can make the setting even more exceptional.

DESIGN TIPS FOR PAVILIONS

- Be generous with the footprint. A space at least 16 by 20 feet will comfortably hold a group seating or a dining table for 12.
- A finished floor isn't absolutely essential, but it helps, especially if it's nice stone or ceramic tile on a slab rather than brick pavers or rough-hewn stone. The tone should lean more to formal than casual.
- Keep the sides as open as possible, with screens or sidewalls no more than waist high. If you do need privacy, keep screening to one or two sides, or use retractable curtains.
- Avoid dark colors. For respite from sun and hot temperatures, lighter colors are preferable.

With a footprint less than 10 feet across, this simple pavilion is about the smallest structure that can lay claim to the name. With its built-in benches, it functions as a seating arbor but offers more protection than an arbor would.

Perched like a private retreat at the edge of a deck, this pavilion features sliding glass doors and full-length curtains that can be drawn to create a separate room. When the doors and curtains are open, the pavilion flows easily into the deck.

When sited properly and fitted with protective features such as screens, pavilions can function as centers for dining and other outdoor activities. The screen fabric darkens the interior somewhat, but the pavilion still feels like an airy outdoor space.

🌼 About Pavilions

Just as other garden structures have signature forms and features but plenty of variations, pavilions often depart from the tried-and-true version of four posts and a roof. The pyramidal roof shape doesn't change much (although flat roofs are a legitimate alternative), but occasionally the lower part of the structure is more complex or ornate, perhaps featuring screens, floor-to-ceiling windows, or French doors.

Look at multiple examples of pavilions and you'll discover that, despite their singular shape, they provide varying degrees of shelter. The structures occupy a spectrum ranging from wide-open frames to a cozy enclosure that keeps wind and weather away. There's no rule that says pavilions can't stray from the original formula and take on a little more protective gear. What's critical is that you maintain open sight lines, which often limits fixed wall materials to transparent screens or glass. Sliding or bifold panels are a great solution because they let you adjust the exposure of the structure to the outdoors, deterring wind-blown rain but giving you a more open space when the weather turns friendly. Flexible features such as these make a pavilion more versatile.

With its additional columns, conventional entry door, and screens, this pavilion stretches the concept to its limits. Any more enclosure and it would seem more like a small building than a garden structure. The brick paver approach and white paint give it a formal look that's classic for a pavilion.

Ramadas

Outdoor structures unique to a particular culture have developed in some regions. One of the most distinctive is the ramada, a staple of Southwestern landscapes.

Of Spanish origin these rustic structures migrated with other cultural elements when Spain brought its colonial ambitions to the Americas. Today they are common in the desert Southwest, and their rustic look mixes effortlessly with adobe architecture.

Ramadas basically are covered porches along the side of the house (logically most often the south side) that provide shade for people sitting outdoors and shade for the house itself, keeping the interior cooler.

They usually have a rustic Spanish flavor that suits many home styles found in western states. Rough-hewn timbers or peeled log posts are common for structural support, and a finish is often absent or inconspicuous,

typically used only for minimal weather protection or to add color intensity. The roof can be closed or feature a simple open framework suggestive of a pergola, and the color palette consists largely of earth tones—golds, reds, and browns that blend with desert landscapes. Detailing is often limited to blocky wood carving, and joinery techniques include rope-tied connections and wood pegs. The tone is one of quaint and no-frills craftsmanship that's compatible with a frontier environment and is the perfect complement to native and other drought-tolerant plantings.

Nothing but peeled logs built into an adobe fireplace wall, this ramada reduces the concept to its bare minimum. Here the purpose is largely to reinforce the authentic Southwest style, but fabric or shade cloth panels could be used to provide protection from the sun.

Nearly silhouetted by a low sun, this structure reveals its kinship with pergolas. It's mostly the materials—rough-sawn lumber, stucco, and terra-cotta paver tiles—that make the ramada label work here. A mister installed at the top of the structure keeps the area comfortable even on the hottest days.

Screened Spaces

In many regions outdoor living is, well, unlivable much of the summer. When you sit outside to enjoy the lovely weather, mosquitoes, flies, and other annoying insects soon send you scurrying for cover.

Enter the screened space. Screened porches have been a favorite for centuries, but screening a roofed structure in the yard can be just as effective. Screened enclosures allow air circulation and keep views mostly intact, while they save you from having to slap gorged mosquitoes on your arms and legs or swat bugs away from your barbecued ribs.

Because closed roof and floor are part of the bug-free package, gazebos and pavilions provide a reliable point of departure for creating a screened building. As long as there's a reasonable framework in place, you can fit individual panels made from aluminum or fiberglass screen fabric in a lightweight wood or metal frame similar to a window screen. If you don't mind a small loss of air movement and slightly decreased visibility, heavier fiberglass screen fabric provides more privacy and better durability; it's often sold as pet screen because it resists tears from dogs and cats. Whatever the type, screens give you more opportunity to enjoy your yard or garden in peace. They also deter birds from building their nests under the roof.

Waterfront settings are ideal breeding grounds for insects, making a space with screens especially appreciated during the summer. If the structure is built on a wood deck, be sure to attach the screen fabric to the underside of the floor planking to close off the gaps.

Outdoor dining structures benefit greatly from insect screens. With standard screen fabric there's little loss of light—and keeping flying insects out reduces health risks and makes mealtime much more enjoyable.

MAKING SCREENS

There are essentially three different ways to build screens into outdoor structures.

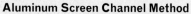

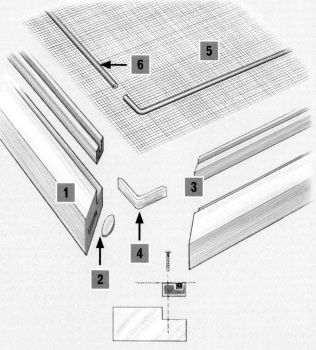

Traditional Screen Frame Construction

Make the wood frame, then staple screen fabric to the frame, stretching it tightly. Cut the excess screen fabric with a utility knife.

1. 1x frame stock
2. ¼×¾-inch screen molding (miter the corners)
3. Fiberglass or other screening material
4. ¾-inch galvanized brads

Aluminum Screen Channel Method

This technique requires some help from a local hardware store or glass shop that makes custom window screens with aluminum channel frames. Just tell the company what sizes you need. To be sure about the sizes, build the wood frames first, then order the screens.

1. 1x frame with rabbeted edge
2. Mitered corners with biscuit joints
3. Aluminum window screen channel
4. Aluminum corner connectors
5. Fiberglass screen fabric
6. Rubber spline

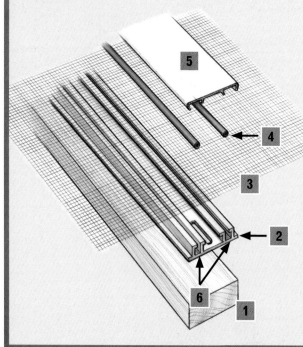

Screen Tight System

This manufactured screen system features extruded vinyl tracks that attach to wood subframes with screws, providing a ready-made channel for the screen fabric and splines. You'll get initial tension when the spline is pressed into place, then the trim cap snaps on and locks it tight.

1. 1×2 wood frame stock
2. Black vinyl screen tight track, attached by screwing to wood frame
3. Fiberglass screen fabric
4. Rubber spline
5. White vinyl trim cap
6. Spline grooves (use one for end frame; both for center frame, brace)

Screened Spaces

Even when an outdoor structure is built with an open frame, retrofitting screened panels is often a relatively simple matter. The first step is to close in the roof if that's not already done: A conventional sheathing-and-shingles design, standing-seam metal, or corrugated roofing panels are three common and practical options. You could use screen overhead, but it's prone to damage and to collecting debris, and it won't provide much shade or protection from rain.

Once the roof is covered, assess the structure's lower frame to make sure there's consistent support for attaching screen frames and to find any small gaps that need closing. Open areas should be limited to about 4 feet wide (wider screen panels are difficult to tension), so on wide wall sections plan for multiple panels and install any intermediate frame braces or supports beforehand.

Standard options for making and fitting screen panels include the traditional wood frame method, aluminum channel frames designed for window screens, and Screen Tight, a system with snap-fit components. These three methods are shown on the opposite page. Recently another manufacturer introduced a retractable screen system that can be installed on most structures and operated manually or electrically.

Aside from the obvious benefit of keeping insects and birds out of your garden structure, screens filter sunlight and increase privacy. This poolside screened pavilion could double as a sleeping porch on warm summer nights.

Teahouses

Whether your goal is to drink tea or simply to sit and contemplate life, an Asian-inspired teahouse provides the ideal serene setting.

Eastern-style garden structures of all types hold appeal for their graceful proportions, skilled joinery, and curved or flared rooflines. Teahouses, called chashitsu in Japan, are especially intriguing. Still a rarity in North American landscapes outside the Pacific Northwest, teahouses exude a tranquility that is welcome in almost any garden. Their often diminutive scale makes it possible for even homeowners with smaller yards to include and enjoy them.

This kind of garden and structure design is a specialty, with expertise that might be hard to find except in major cities or areas with a significant Asian population. If you don't have any luck through referrals or phone book listings, check with a regional arboretum or with local garden centers that supply landscape architects and installers. Also books and Internet forums on Asian-style gardens are widely available, so even if local landscape contractors or builders don't have much experience with the particulars you can find readily available resources to help in the planning and design.

Expect to spend more for these exotic structures than you would an ordinary pergola or pavilion. The complex roof shapes, shoji screens, and other elements require a lot of time and skill to make. It's time and effort well spent.

Eastern-inspired gardens excel at providing a feeling of sanctuary and seclusion, and this tea house-inspired pavilion offers a stellar example of that aesthetic. The craftsmanship is deliberate and detailed but doesn't overpower the inherent quality of the materials or the setting.

Asian-style structures work best in the proper context, which means the garden should feature consistent design elements throughout. Here a zigzag bridge (believed to thwart evil spirits) and a stone-edge pond provide the right setting for a pavilion. The structure isn't enclosed with shoji screens like a traditional teahouse, but the roof ridge and ornate wood trim clearly indicate its Eastern roots.

THE TEA CEREMONY

The formal tea ceremony is so highly ritualized that it can take years of study to learn. Still the spirit of the ceremony can be a part of your garden experience.

Although other Asian cultures have their own versions, Japanese and Chinese tea ceremonies are said to have evolved from Zen Buddhist traditions. It isn't a religious experience the way churchgoers in the Western world think of religion, but it is very much a spiritual exercise.

Think of the tea ceremony as a deliberately intense experience of ordinary everyday things. Each step in the process is done with great care as if to honor and elevate mundane tasks and humble items to a sacred role. Simple utensils are carefully washed and arranged. A minimalist floral arrangement sits in a handmade ceramic vase. Water is patiently boiled, then poured over tea leaves. This focus on disciplined and reverent action is key, and the experience of being "in the present moment" is not only a central tenet of Zen traditions but a great attitude for enjoying time in your garden.

Incorporating Fabric

Fabrics play a central role in most interior decor schemes, but they're often overlooked when it comes to the outdoors. That's unfortunate because they add color, texture, and softness that can make an outdoor structure truly inviting and comfortable, giving it the feel of a genuine living space.

Of course there's always been a drawback to using fabrics outside, especially when the choices were limited to cotton, linen, and other natural materials. Repeated exposure to rain, snow, wind, and direct sunlight quickly ruins most natural fabrics, but today there are alternatives designed specifically for outdoor use. They tend to be heavier, and newer generations are acrylic blends designed to be more colorfast, water resistant, and mildew resistant than natural fibers.

Standard uses for outdoor fabrics include awnings, patio umbrellas, and furniture cushions, but why limit yourself to the ordinary? Any opening in a structure can be treated like a window or doorway, something to be embellished or accented with flowing draperies, a valance, or a colorful shade. These applications have a practical value as well; much more than rigid components made of wood or metal, fabrics offer an easy way to change a structure in response to weather patterns or other circumstances.

Low afternoon sun getting a little intense? Just unfurl a tied drapery and let it provide shade instantly where you need it. Want to convert your pergola from sunny and open to a secluded dining space? A few inconspicuous hooks can provide support for fabric panels that enclose the sides and create plenty of privacy.

Fabrics can even offer seasonal variety. While the posts and beams of your structure remain the same over the years, fabrics can be easily changed to reflect your evolving taste or to suit your mood. No other accessory can do as much for so little.

Fabrics have plenty of practical value for outdoor structures. The full-length curtains on this pavilion tie back to let air and sunshine in, but they can be closed for shelter if wind or cooler temperatures threaten to spoil the party.

Fabric can be an accessory to an outdoor structure or, as in this case, part of the structure itself. Guy wires steady temporary posts that help support a simple awning. Requiring only minutes to put up or take down, the awning serves as a staging point for floral displays and a shady spot to make the garden bench more inviting.

The tied draperies here show how fabric's contribution of color and curves can relieve the stark geometry of most garden structures, creating a much more relaxing and welcoming space. Even if your fabric choices aren't designed for outdoor use, arrangements such as this can be taken down easily when they're not needed.

Garden Structures With Fireplaces

Fireplaces are as appealing and romantic out of doors as they are inside a home, so it's no surprise they are an increasingly popular feature for garden structures. Live flames still entrance us, and as a heat source a fireplace can extend the usable season for an outdoor space. But as ancient and simple as it is, the appeal of fire introduces some serious complexities into modern building projects.

First there are legal issues, because some cities, counties, and even homeowner associations don't allow woodburning outdoor fireplaces. And those that do often closely regulate their design and use. In some areas the restrictions involve air quality rather than fire safety, so even the safest design and installation may not be legal. Also the decision to include a fireplace affects the materials you need for your structure and perhaps the contractor you hire to build it.

Traditional masonry construction using mortared stone or brick is still a favorite technique, but modular metal fireplaces and gas-burning inserts now offer more options.

Wood decks and fireplaces normally don't mix, but some freestanding metal or ceramic units (such as chimineas) can be used if noncombustible surfaces and materials are installed to insulate the deck from excess heat.

Beyond the legal and practical issues are aesthetic and functional ones. An outdoor fireplace should be central to the setting in the same way that an interior hearth is. Place furniture groupings or built-in benches comfortably and naturally around or near it, close enough for you and your guests to enjoy the warmth. If possible build in a dry firewood storage bay and perhaps plan on a wide hearth ledge to double as extra seating. If your home's location doesn't introduce legal obstacles to an outdoor fireplace, this is one feature likely to encourage more use of a pavilion or other large garden structure.

Masonry fireplaces can add significantly to the cost of an outdoor structure, but their value and appeal are undeniable. This stone version sits at the edge of the pavilion to allow the chimney an easy vertical exit yet is still within close range of the seating group.

This gorgeous pavillion is more like a pool house with enclosed private areas, but what makes it really special is the fireplace, which allows you to take in views of the pond even during cool mountain and autumn evenings.

OUTDOOR FIREPLACE CODES

Before investing in design work or materials for an outdoor fireplace, check with your city or county officials to make sure you can build a legal one on your property. Here are some common regulations you need to know about:

- Some cities and counties prohibit any and all outdoor fireplaces, for either air quality or fire safety concerns, or sometimes both.
- Where allowed most fireplaces must meet established code specifications for appropriate materials, the size of the firebox opening, minimum clearance to combustible materials, proper venting and drafting, hearth extension, and seismic reinforcement (in earthquake-prone areas). Never assume your design will pass inspection; get the plans approved before any work is done.
- Chimneys that pass through roofs or are near other buildings require a minimum height above the roofline, often referred to as the 10/2/3 rule: Any part of a structure within 10 horizontal feet of a chimney top must be at least 2 feet above the cap, and the chimney must extend at least 3 feet above the roof surface it abuts or penetrates. (Ask local officials to see if this rule applies in your case.)
- Skirting code restrictions may invalidate your homeowner's insurance coverage in the event of a fire, so stay within the law.

The typically open roof of a portico allows ample daylight into an entryway, which a solid roof might make oppressively dark. It makes the approach pleasantly shaded though still airy.

MAKING A MEMORABLE ENTRANCE

- Keep the scale appropriate for the house. Too small or too large and it will be a misfit in a prominent place.
- Scale it appropriately. It's a common error to build too heavy an entry structure. Lighter or simpler structures can be like jewels on a house, noticeable for their differences.
- Finish it with a trim color, not the main color of the house. This lets the structure read visually as an accessory or accent.
- Don't skimp on quality of materials or craftsmanship. Keep in mind that aside from a quick glance from curbside, this is the first statement your house makes to visitors and guests.

Porticos and Entries

Garden structures don't always have to be in the backyard. When pergolas relocate from the back to the front, however, they get a new name—portico—and a slightly different function.

A portico shares the open-frame anatomy common to most garden structures, but it sits at a home's front entry rather than in a rear or side yard. It isn't a gathering place the way a pergola is meant to be, but rather an ornamental feature to draw attention to the entry and to add architectural interest. As with most accessory structures attached directly to a home, it needs to share some elements—trim color or millwork details, for example—in order to appear integrated with its host building.

Porticos are especially useful as substitutes for front porches, mainly because they typically cost far less to build. Yet they serve essentially the same function. Although a portico is lighter and less substantial, it still announces the home's entrance to visitors.

A portico is also less common than a porch and when innovatively designed it can add a touch of style and surprise to a front entry.

A portico gives a sense of shelter to an otherwise exposed entry. Even though it extends only a few feet to the front steps, this structure forges a nice transition between indoors and out, and the lattice panels create an airy look suitable for a garden setting.

Porticos and Entries

Porticos are the perfect (and not very expensive) solution to ho-hum entries or those entries that don't have enough importance—the ones that you look at twice to make sure they're really the right way to get into the house.

Porticos serve much the same function as a front porch. They announce the front entry and welcome visitors, but they're not as extensive.

Some porticos are fairly fancy, but it's easy to keep things simple by attaching the overhead portico frame to the exterior wall or the roof fascia so only one or two posts are needed for support. Be sure to connect the ledger to the wall or roof framing, not merely to siding, sheathing, or the thin fascia board.

On some older homes with driveways right next to the house, it's common to see porticos built around side entries. The posts are kept wide of the driveway to allow vehicles to pass, and the overhead frame can be left open like a pergola or sheathed and roofed for more protection from the weather.

Finally keep in mind that you can use trellis panels or climbing plants, or both, to embellish a simple entry structure or provide more shade. Aim for charm and a sense of welcome.

Entries without porch roofs or other embellishments can seem stark and barren, especially on modest homes that have few interesting features. Fitting a simple pergola-style structure like this one can add definition and make the house seem more welcoming.

Inconspicuous front entries are easier to identify if they are highlighted by a portico or similar structure. Tucked into a corner and surrounded by foliage, this home's entry door would be hard to spot on its own. Adding the portico sends the eye, and any visitors, in the right direction.

Lath Houses

A close look at the garden structures in this book reveals that they all vary in exactly how much of the outdoors they allow in. A screened pavilion with a solid roof says "enclosure," while a wide-open pergola creates a suggestion of shelter that's greater than the protection it actually provides. Somewhere in between these polar opposites is the lath house.

A lath house typically features some sort of structural frame covered by narrow strips of wood (called lath) rather than roofing shingles, siding, or screens. The lath patterns can vary from simple parallel lines to diagonal mesh or square grids, but the effect is consistent. Numerous small openings in the roof and walls, usually at least the size of the lath itself, allow air and light to move through the structure relatively freely.

For greater privacy space the lath closer together or use manufactured lattice panels. However porous the final result, lath houses provide a great visual texture that isn't found in other types of outdoor structures.

With an open grid that seems to suggest window muntins, this lath house keeps views relatively clear. Note that the lath pattern on the roof is linear and much tighter than on the walls, a common feature.

With a hip roof reminiscent of an old railroad depot platform, this structure has lath spaced densely enough to provide substantial shade. A small enclosure like this provides a comfortable nesting spot even though the shelter it provides from rain or cold temperatures is minimal.

Side Yard Solutions

In many landscapes the side yard is a wasted space just waiting to be transformed. It may be little more than a narrow alley leading from the back to the front, or it may be amazingly spacious. Either way it is too often overlooked, especially since it is frequently hidden away from easy sight, making it perfect for a private garden space.

A garden structure can transform a side yard. Often side yards are shady places where plant choices are limited, restricting what you can grow there. But a structure can add instant garden charm, making even a narrow side yard a place you'll want to linger.

Some side yards are primarily entry areas. These too can be transformed with a structure, adding importance to the entry and turning what might be a bleak spot into a pretty space that welcomes you home after a long day.

Other side yards are primarily narrow strips that allow you to travel between the front and back of your property.

Even if you have room for little more than a path, a good-looking arbor or gate marking either end makes for a pleasant journey.

If your side yard is more of a utility area, perhaps housing garbage cans, the kids' bikes, and other less-than-attractive accoutrements of modern living, consider screening them with a trellis or fence and recreate the remainder of the space into a more aesthetic area.

In narrow lots privacy can be a concern. A fence will block views from the side, and an arbor or pergola will screen the view from above if you're concerned about neighbors looking down from second-story windows.

The long sectional trellis creates a useful zone for potting benches and gardening work, affording some privacy and providing a staging area for an assortment of potted flowering plants. It's also neighbor-friendly, keeping project clutter and unsightly equipment out of view.

This nicely proportioned gate-and-arbor duo is offset to the side, allowing guests to bypass the home's front entry and head straight to the backyard. The structure provides virtually the same privacy and security as a fence but offers more versatility and charm.

Narrow areas don't always mean there's no room to build. Here an ensemble of three structures—a small-grid trellis, a larger L-shape trellis for privacy, and a gated arbor—all fit in a side yard that's only several feet wide.

WHAT SIDE YARD STRUCTURES CAN DO

- Carve out a niche for relaxation
- Create a smooth transition between the front yard and backyard
- Provide shade and/or privacy for a side entry to the house
- Act as a background or support for plants
- Camouflage air-conditioning units or garbage cans
- Create a containment area for pets
- Secure the backyard against unauthorized entry

Sometimes side yards can be more than transitional areas between front and back landscapes. Here a shallow pergola and sectional stone patio create small alcoves for dining or entertaining. The pergola's small scale might limit the group size, but the setting is inviting and comfortable.

Side Yard Solutions

With all but the smallest garden structures your first step is to check local building codes. Often regulations determine how high you can construct a fence and other structures in a side yard as well as how close to the property line you can locate them.

If you're part of a homeowners association, you'll also need to check with the governing body to make sure your plans conform with neighborhood regulations. Residents of historic districts might have to meet certain design and building rules too.

When building a structure alongside your house, note any utility connections such as supply lines and meters for natural gas, water, or electrical cables. Many of these connections are made at a home's sidewalls, which means pipes and wiring may be buried. You'll have to avoid them in digging holes for post footings. Most counties and cities offer free underground utility locating services; call to arrange a site inspection before you dig.

Remember too that side yards sometimes are the only means of access for heavy equipment to fenced backyards. If that's true of your yard, keep access in mind as you design fences, gates, and other structures that might block lawn mowers or, in case of any large-scale home project, a small backhoe or other heavy equipment.

The key to side yard privacy isn't necessarily to obstruct the view entirely but merely to screen views. In this case the grid trellis interrupts the sight line while the lush plantings demand attention up front. Only the light through the gateway pulls the eye into the yard.

What might have been merely a utilitarian path to a greenhouse serves instead as an arbor and a display area for more than a dozen flowering plants. A retaining wall behind the wood structure helps handle the pressure from the terraced slope.

FINDING THE RIGHT SIDE YARD SOLUTION

Because no single design fits all landscapes, any side yard projects you want should be tailored to the specifics of your site.

Here are four typical side yard layouts with suggestions on how to transform them into something special with the help of garden structures. Even if the individual projects don't transfer exactly to your yard, they can inspire similar solutions that will work for you.

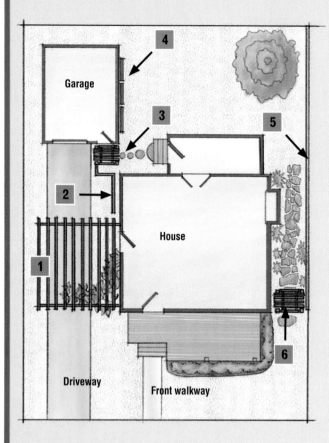

House With Detached Garage in Rear

1. Pergola over the driveway and side entrance to provide an attractive focal point and also shade and modest protection from the elements

2. Privacy trellis to block views from neighbors

3. Gated arbor to add architectural interest and provide a sense of arrival into the garden area

4. Wall-mounted trellis to visually soften the side of the garage

5. Privacy trellis or fence to block views and for a welcome sense of enclosure

6. Gated arbor to give a sense of arrival and welcome to the modest stone path area

Suburban Home With Front Attached Garage

1. Portico structure to add importance and a sense of welcome to the front door and also direct traffic through the narrow side yard

2. Arbor gate for architectural interest, to clearly mark the side yard as a place worth entering, and to keep pets and children in the backyard

3. Tunnel arbor to create an enchanting journey through the side yard

4. Flagstone patio off the French doors to help marry the space between indoors and out

5. Low fence to enclose the yard yet still allow easy interaction with neighbors and also clearly delineate the property

6. Corner trellis, 6 feet high, to provide privacy and a feeling of enclosure that the low fence cannot

7. Second gate to allow easy access to tools in the garage but also seal the backyard

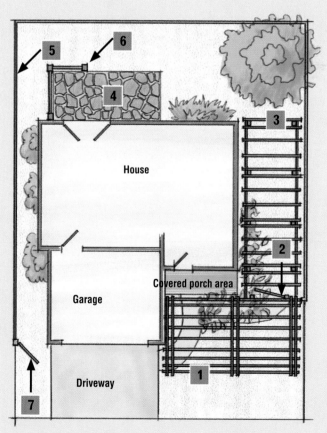

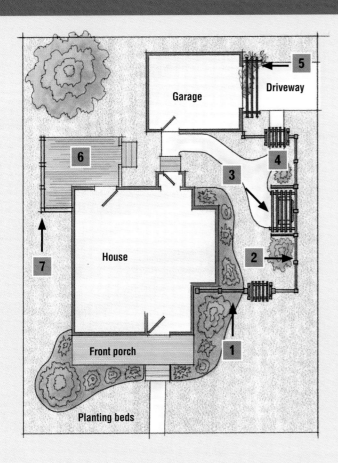

Corner Lot With Detached Garage

1. Privacy trellis to screen views without being oppressive

2. Tall fence solid on the bottom two-thirds for privacy and latticework on the top one-third to make it more inviting than a completely solid fence

3. Seating arbor to create a sense of destination and a focal point in the landscape

4. Gated arbor matching the seating arbor to give the homeowners a welcoming entrance to the landscape after work

5. Shallow vine-planted pergola over the garage to visually soften the architecture and shade a sun-baked area

6. Deck to create a transition between outdoors and indoors and provide a spot for dining and relaxing

7. L-shape privacy trellis planted with vines to screen views and wind

Corner Lot With Storage Shed

1. Trellis to provide privacy without being oppressive

2. Arbor gate to draw in visitors from the front and provide access from the front to the back

3. Potting bench to add storage and utility to an otherwise vacant space

4. Long, tall trellis fence for some privacy without closing off the space completely

5. Brick walk to add more substance to the area as well as solid footing in wet weather

6. Concrete patio with brick inlay to provide outdoor living space and for visual tie-in with the walk

7. Gazebo to create an outdoor room ideal for dining

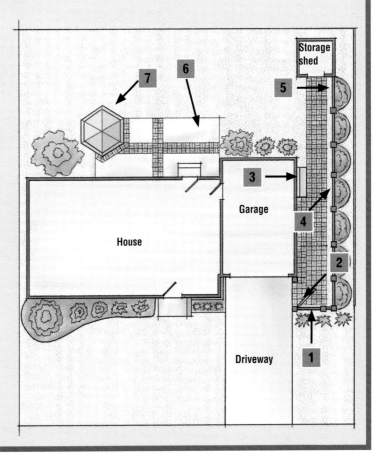

Whimsical Garden Structures

What's that you say? No category seems right? No garden structure seems to contain the elusive blend of personality and purpose that you want? Just because you haven't found it yet doesn't mean that it doesn't or shouldn't exist. If you've imagined it, you can work to make it happen.

Sometimes the definitions and distinctions don't matter and all you want is something that grabs your gut. Your perfect garden structure might be nonsensical or outlandish or wonderfully understated, or simply something unexpected. There are plenty of examples of hybrid designs and classic forms, but some structures just defy simple explanations or push past normal limits to become something special. The structures shown here are just a few of the renegade possibilities that someone imagined when no real version existed. If you haven't settled on your design yet, these might give your creative power just the nudge it needs.

Screens doors hinged together and topped with a fabric canopy make this structure portable, making it easy to store indoors come fall. A roll-down screen in the front make it a perfect nook for an afternoon nap or even a night of sleeping under the stars.

(Top left) This beautifully crafted rustic entrance likely doesn't feature a single straight line. Inspired by the woods surrounding it, this entrance uses materials taken directly from nature. (Top right) This fabulous metal onion-domed structure is a magical place to enjoy friends and meals. It also provides practical suport for the climbing roses surrounding it.

(Bottom left) This sitting area is sheltered from the elements but otherwise essentially open. Latticework pieces flanking either side help it blend with the fence behind it and give it more importance.

(Bottom right) With a charming roof that suggests a centuries-old European cottage and substantial walls that are partly lattice, this small garden house keeps out wind and rain but allows cooling breezes.

Vines for Garden Structures

One of the best things about outdoor structures is that they can function as supports for luxuriant vines.

A pergola, for example, may look a little stark unless it's cloaked in shade-providing vines. And some garden structures such as arbors and trellises are made specifically to support vines.

But all vines are not created equal. Some grow more thickly than others. Some are rampant—climbing to 60 feet—and will not just cover an arbor but obliterate it. Most vines do best in full sun (at least 6 hours of direct, unfiltered light at day), but a handful do well in shade. Others grow fast to quickly add greenery; still others have beautiful flowers and perhaps even a wonderful fragrance.

How a vine climbs is also important. Many simply twine upward while others send out tendrils that latch onto supports. Either type is ideal for outdoor structures.

Beware vines that grab on with adhesive disks or tiny rootlet systems. While some homeowners like the fact that these vines attach themselves to permanent surfaces such as stone or brick, such vines are problematic on wood or stucco siding—they're difficult to remove when you want to repaint. The little disks and rootlets tend to tear away, leaving hundreds of bits of plant material on the building that need to be scraped or sanded away.

On brick and other mortared surfaces, these fairly permanent plantings are acceptable as long as the mortar is in excellent shape. Otherwise these tenacious vines might work their way into even hairline cracks and crevices and worsen them.

But perhaps the most important factor in deciding what vine to plant with your garden structure is the size of the vine. Read the plant label carefully—and then believe it. Many homeowners have planted vines labeled as growing to 40 feet on 7-foot-tall arbors, not believing it could possibly get that large, only to rip it out four or five years later. Choose a vine that's the right size for your structure.

DECIDING ON THE RIGHT VINE

These are some things you should keep in mind when shopping for a vine.
- Is it an annual, which has to be replanted every year, or is it a perennial?
- Does it need shade or sun?
- Does it like wet conditions or dry?
- How large does it grow and how quickly?
- Does it have flowers or berries?
- Is it fragrant?
- How does it climb? Does it need a special support? Does it need to be tied to the structure?

Morning glories are the classic fast-growing annual vine. They can be slow to start (be sure to soak the seeds overnight first) but once started, can quickly cover even the largest structures.

HOW VINES CLIMB

Different vines climb upward in different ways. Knowing which ones use which method will help you choose the perfect vine to ascend your structure.

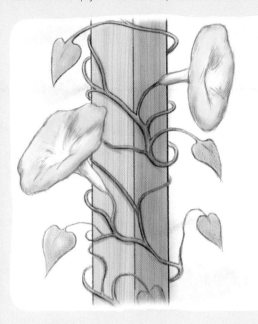

Twining Vines
These vines have long, usually pliable stems that twine upward around a string, pole, or post as they grow. They are easy to cut down and seldom damage structures.

Clinging Tendrils
Some vines produce tendrils that reach out until they grab hold of a support. They do best on structures with a grid such as latticework; it's more difficult for them to climb a smooth post or pole.

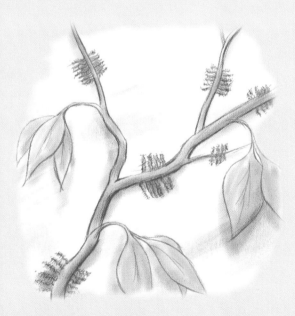

Clinging Aerial Rootlets
A handful of vines cling to surfaces by putting out tiny rootlets that hold tightly to surfaces. The rootlets are so tenacious they can climb nearly anything but are best used on stucco, brick, and other surfaces that don't need frequent maintenance.

Adhesive Disks
Also called holdfasts these suction cuplike disks attach themselves very securely. Like aerial rootlets they are very difficult to remove to maintain a surface and are so tough that they may need to be sanded off. Acceptable on mortared and stucco surfaces.

🌸 A Gallery of Vines

AMERICAN BITTERSWEET
Celastrus scandens

A native American vine frequently spotted growing wild in sunny, open areas, bittersweet is loved for its bright orange and red berries in fall.

Large and somewhat invasive, the vine develops slender, trunklike stems at its base and can grow well over 20 feet with a twining, rather sprawling habit. Plant it where its loose twining will be at home, such as atop a sturdy pergola. The vine often sends up suckers, sometimes several feet from the main plant. Plant a male and a female plant to ensure berry development.

Full sun to light shade. Drought tolerant. Cold hardy to as much as –30°F.

BOUGAINVILLEA
Bougainvillea

These gorgeous vines cloak entire buildings in the warmest climates. Their true flowers are surrounded by gorgeous colored bracts in red, orange, coral, peach, white, magenta, pink, or purple. Depending on the variety, the vine may be able to tolerate the lightest of frosts with some protection, but as a rule bougainvillea thrives in frost-free areas. In colder climates plants are sometimes available in pots but are intended to last just one growing season.

Needs full sun, though thrives in light shade in the hottest areas. Grows 20 to 40 feet tall, depending on variety. Climbs by leaning and grabbing with its long thorns. Should also be tied to the supporting structure.

Hardy in areas with little or no frost. In other parts of the country, however, often sold to grow for just one year or as a temporary indoor plant.

CLEMATIS

The three most commonly grown types, described here, all climb by twining.

Hybrid Clematis
Clematis × *hybrida*

These are the most popular clematis, the ones with stems that don't get particularly tall and have beautiful large flowers in blue, purple, pink, red, white, and bicolors. Many of the hybrids bloom nonstop from early summer to fall. Some have two flushes of bloom, in spring and fall.

The various hybrids grow 8 to 12 feet. Help the vine along by twisting the stems on the support. A vine may also need to be lightly tied. Clematis vines like their heads in the sun and their feet in the shade, as the old saying goes, so mulch or plant perennials or annuals at their bases. Rich, moist, well-drained soil. Some are cold hardy to as much as –30°F.

Armand Clematis
Clematis armandii

This clematis features leathery dark green leaves forked into three leaflets. Although attractive year round, it's especially nice in early spring when it bears masses of almond-scented, 2-inch white flowers. The vine grows 20 to 30 feet.

Full sun to part shade, especially in southern regions. Rich, well-drained soil. Cold hardy to 0°F.

Sweet Autumn Clematis
Usually sold as *Clematis paniculata*

In late summer this vigorous vine covers itself with tiny cream-colored flowers with the heavenly heavy scent of honey. It grows quickly, as much as 10 feet in one year, and ultimately reaches 20 to 30 feet.

Full sun to light shade. Prefers rich, well-drained soil but is somewhat drought tolerant. Cold hardy to as much as –30°F.

FIVE-LEAF AKEBIA
Akebia quinata

In cooler regions this twining vine is relatively well behaved, hitting perhaps 20 feet with fanlike leaves with five rounded leaflets with reddish stems. In warmer regions where the plant is evergreen, it can reach 30 feet and produce heavy greenery and sprays of small rosy flowers that don't look like much but have a lovely spicy vanilla or chocolate scent. Also in warm climates, where the growing season is longer, fat purple pods form in late fall. Since this fast-growing vine can grow 10 to 15 feet the first season, it's excellent quick color for a garden structure.

Full sun to full shade, but most rampant in sun. Will be smaller and less dense in shade, which can be a good thing since this vine often is invasive in warm areas. Prefers rich, moist, well-drained soil. Cold hardy to –30°F.

CLIMBING ROSES

The many different kinds of climbing roses range from miniature climbers that grow just 6 feet to ramblers that can reach 40 feet or more. Most roses are cold hardy to as much as –20°F. Just a handful are more cold hardy than that.

Rambler Roses

Aptly named, these roses can attain giant proportions, roaming 30 to 40 feet high and covering a tree or even a small house. Most bloom just once a year and are very cold hardy and disease resistant. Some of the best known include the lady banks rose (Rosa banksiae 'Lutea') and 'Paul's Himalayan Musk Rambler'.

Large-flowered Climbing Roses

Nearly any rose that grows more than 8 to 10 feet can be trained as a climber, but those with fairly upright canes lend themselves more to the role than those with sprawling canes. Large-flowered climbing roses usually grow 15 to 20 feet, depending on the climate. Most are not hardy beyond –20°F (though 'William Baffin' and 'Henry Kelsey' are notable exceptions) and are not absolutely reliably hard beyond –10°F. Some of the best known climbers are 'Blaze', 'New Dawn', 'Joseph's Coat', 'America', and 'Dortmund'.

Pillar Roses

These are the roses with an upright habit that grow perhaps just 8 to 10 feet tall, making them suitable for attaching to posts and small trellises. They lack the long, usually flexible canes of climbers and ramblers and therefore need extra help with careful tying to the support. Popular roses for growing on pillars, posts, and other small supports include 'Flutterbye', 'Paul's Lemon Pillar', 'Altissimo', and 'Dream Weaver'.

Miniature Climbing Roses

Also try one of the miniature climbers, fairly new to the market (shown is 'Jeanne Lajoie'.) These beauties climb up to 6 feet and cover themselves with perfect, tiny roses.

HONEYSUCKLE
Lonicera spp.

Rampant but popular twining vines, honeysuckles can cover entire fences or trellises in a year or two.

Goldflame honeysuckle (*L. × heckrottiis*) sprawls about 10 feet high and wide. The fragrant flowers feature two colors: pink and yellow. The foliage is evergreen in warm climates.

Japanese honeysuckle (*L. japonica*) is a profuse grower with tiny, highly fragrant creamy white flowers in early summer. The plant reaches 30 feet high and is semi-evergreen in warmer climates. In late summer to early autumn it produces black berries that birds love.

Trumpet honeysuckle (*L. sempervirens*) has bright scarlet flowers on plants that grow to 25 feet high. The flowers are scentless but are beloved by hummingbirds. Plants sometimes produce red berries in fall. This species is classified as a noxious weed in the Southeast.

All honeysuckles need full sun to light shade and like rich, well-drained but moist soil. Rampant growers are less vigorous in drier soils and shadier spots. Cold hardy to as much as −30°F.

JASMINE, COMMON
Jasminum officinale

Gorgeously fragrant tiny white flowers appear in abundance in early summer and continue lightly through fall, perfuming an entire corner of the garden. The vine can reach as high as 30 feet; its leaves are deciduous in cold climates and semi-evergreen in warmer ones. Full sun. Moist, average, well-drained soil. Cold hardy to 20°F.

JASMINE, STAR
Trachelospermum jasminoides

Also called confederate jasmine. Sometimes sold in cold-winter areas as a short-lived houseplant or an annual vine, this twining warm-climate favorite produces tons of sweetly scented tiny white star-shape flowers in early summer. The plant gets just 6 to 8 feet high and has lustrous, slightly waxy, dark green oval leaves, making it attractive even when not in flower. Star jasmine is sometimes allowed to sprawl as a groundcover. The similar Asiatic jasmine (*T. asiaticum*) has yellowish blooms.

Part to full shade. Average to rich, well-drained soil. Needs ample moisture. Perennial in areas where winters don't get colder than 10°F.

JESSAMINE, CAROLINA
Gelsemium sempervirens

This native of the South is a twining vine that grows to 20 feet and blooms in late winter and early spring; its small yellow trumpet-shape flowers have a lovely scent. Glossy, pointed green leaves cloak the plant year-round.

Full sun to light shade. Average to rich, well-drained soil with average moisture; drought tolerant once established. Cold hardy to 0°F.

MANDEVILLA
Mandevilla splendens

Often sold in cold-winter regions as a pretty potted annual that will reach 10 feet before being killed by frost, in warm climates mandevilla is an easily managed vine that twines to 30 feet high. It's prized for its lovely 5-inch pink or white flowers produced steadily from spring through fall. The waxy oval leaves are a lustrous dark green.

This tropical native does best in full sun in colder regions and light shade in warmer climates. Needs ample moisture and regular fertilizing for best flowering. Cold hardy to 10°F.

PASSIONFLOWER
Passiflora spp.
This exotic beauty, which climbs with the help of tendrils, is a favorite in very warm climates. It produces 2- to 4-inch brightly colored flowers with showy stamens.

Blue passionflower (*P. caerulea*) bears 4-inch flowers that combine blue, pink, and white and have a slight fragrance. The semi-evergreen to evergreen foliage grows to 30 feet. Cold hardy to 10°F.

Maypop (*P. incarnata*) has pinkish white flowers with purple stamens followed by edible yellow fruits. Cold hardy to 0°F.

Wing-stemmed passionflower (*P. alata*) has fragrant red, purple, and white flowers. Passionfruit (*P. edulus*) bears purple and white flowers that mature into edible fruits. Cold hardy to 10°F.

PYRACANTHA
Pyracantha coccinea
As much a shrub as a vine, pyracantha—sometimes called firethorn—has thorny, long, sprawling branches and produces large flat clusters of white flowers in early summer. But its wonderful bunches of red, orange, or sometimes yellow berries in fall distinguish it. The long, narrow, glossy dark green leaves are evergreen in warmer climates and semi-evergreen in colder areas. Plants are often trained to wires or other supports against a tall wall; the branches must be tied to the support.

Needs full sun and good circulation. Average to poor well-drained soil. Tolerates heat and drought. Cold hardy to as much as −10°F with a few cultivars hardy to as much as −20°F.

SILVER LACE VINE
Polygonum aubertii
This twining vine gets its name from the puffs of pearly white flower clusters it develops in late summer. It has bright green arrow-shape leaves and can hit 20 feet the first season, topping out at around 30 feet. The vine travels by underground stems, which can make it somewhat invasive in ideal or warmer conditions.

Needs full sun to very light shade. Does well in most soils. Cold hardy to as much as −30°F. Dies back to the ground in cold climates.

TRUMPET VINE
Campsis radicans
Somewhat invasive, trumpet vine rapidly climbs any structure including trees and light poles, forming a thick trunklike stem over time. Beautiful clusters of trumpet-shape orange to red flowers bloom for weeks in late summer and are a hummingbird magnet. The leaves are attractive—large, glossy, and dark green.

The vine climbs 40 feet high by means of twining and aerial rootlets, which are difficult to remove for painting and other maintenance and can be destructive to masonry and wood shingles. It often sends up suckers, including ones several feet from the main plant.

Full sun to part shade, but flowering is best in sun. Grows in a variety of soils; poor soil has the benefit of restricting growth. Cold hardy to as much as −30°F.

WISTERIA
Wisteria floribunda
Among the most romantic vines around, wisteria has beautiful fragrant purple or white flower clusters that hang down 1 to 2 feet. In warmer climates wisteria can be a problem because it grows so large (40 feet) with a stem as thick as a tree trunk. The vine, which climbs by twining, needs an extremely solid, large structure. Full sun. Not hardy below −20°F.

VINES TO AVOID ON MOST GARDEN STRUCTURES

The following vines attach themselves with adhesive disks or rootlets that are difficult to remove from structures for painting or maintenance. The disks or rootlets also can wreak havoc with masonry that's not in excellent condition or shingles.

Boston ivy (*Parthenocissus tricuspidat*)
Climbing hydrangea (*Hydrangea petiolaris*)
Virginia creeper (*Parthenocissus quinquefolia*)
Creeping fig (*Ficus pumila*)
English ivy (*Hedera helix*)
Wintercreeper (*Euonymus fortunei*)

FRAGRANT VINES

Some vines give off a great fragrance, especially in late afternoon or early evening. These are some of the best.
• Climbing roses, some types
• Honeysuckle, some types
• Jasmine, all types
• Jessamine, Carolina
• Moonflower
• Passionflower, some types
• Star jasmine
• Sweet autumn clematis
• Sweet pea
• Wisteria, some types

ANNUAL VINES

When you want blossoms within the first year, try flowering annual vines. They're inexpensive, and because most are sold as seeds you can have several plants for less than you'd pay for a cup of coffee.

Nearly all flowering annual vines like full sun and rich, moist, well-drained soil. After your region's last frost date in spring, soak the seeds overnight in warm water and plant them directly in the soil. It may take a few days for them to germinate and even longer to get to any size. All the annual vines listed here grow by twining.

In cold-winter areas expect the vines to reach full size and bloom by midsummer. They'll last a month or two until frost. In warmer climates expect a few to several months of enjoyment. They include:

Black-eyed susan vine (*Thurbergia alata*)
Cardinal climber (*Ipomoea × multifida*)
Hyacinth bean (*Lablab purpureus*)
Morning glory (*Ipomoea tricolor*)
Moonflower (*Ipomoea alba*)
Scarlet runner bean (*Phaseolus coccineus*)
Sweet pea (*Lathyrus odoratus*)

Black-eyed susan vine   Cardinal climber   Hyacinth bean   Morning glory

Moonflower   Scarlet runner bean   Sweet pea

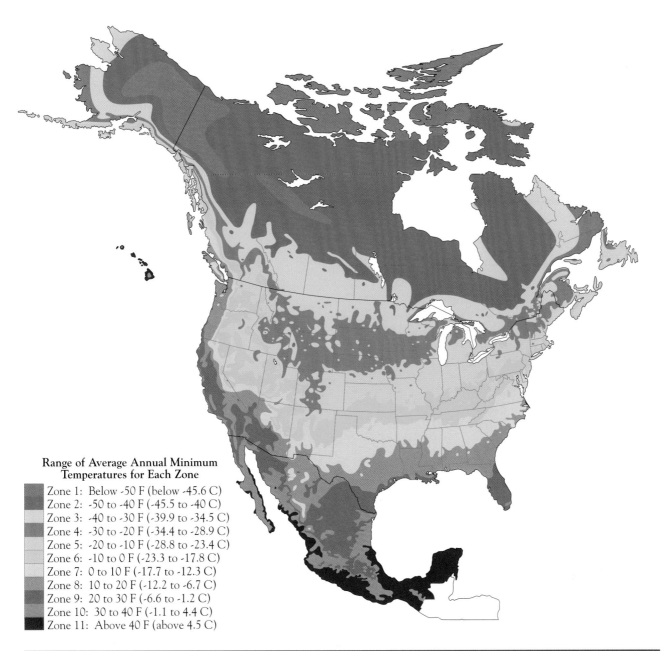

Range of Average Annual Minimum
Temperatures for Each Zone

Zone 1: Below -50 F (below -45.6 C)
Zone 2: -50 to -40 F (-45.5 to -40 C)
Zone 3: -40 to -30 F (-39.9 to -34.5 C)
Zone 4: -30 to -20 F (-34.4 to -28.9 C)
Zone 5: -20 to -10 F (-28.8 to -23.4 C)
Zone 6: -10 to 0 F (-23.3 to -17.8 C)
Zone 7: 0 to 10 F (-17.7 to -12.3 C)
Zone 8: 10 to 20 F (-12.2 to -6.7 C)
Zone 9: 20 to 30 F (-6.6 to -1.2 C)
Zone 10: 30 to 40 F (-1.1 to 4.4 C)
Zone 11: Above 40 F (above 4.5 C)

METRIC CONVERSIONS

U.S. UNITS TO METRIC EQUIVALENTS			METRIC UNITS TO U.S. EQUIVALENTS		
To Convert From	Multiply By	To Get	To Convert From	Multiply By	To Get
Inches	25.4	Millimeters	Millimeters	0.0394	Inches
Inches	2.54	Centimeters	Centimeters	0.3937	Inches
Feet	30.48	Centimeters	Centimeters	0.0328	Feet
Feet	0.3048	Meters	Meters	3.2808	Feet
Yards	0.9144	Meters	Meters	1.0936	Yards
Square inches	6.4516	Square centimeters	Square centimeters	0.1550	Square inches
Square feet	0.0929	Square meters	Square meters	10.764	Square feet
Square yards	0.8361	Square meters	Square meters	1.1960	Square yards
Acres	0.4047	Hectares	Hectares	2.4711	Acres
Cubic inches	16.387	Cubic centimeters	Cubic centimeters	0.0610	Cubic inches
Cubic feet	0.0283	Cubic meters	Cubic meters	35.315	Cubic feet
Cubic feet	28.316	Liters	Liters	0.0353	Cubic feet
Cubic yards	0.7646	Cubic meters	Cubic meters	1.308	Cubic yards
Cubic yards	764.55	Liters	Liters	0.0013	Cubic yards

To convert from degrees Fahrenheit (F) to degrees Celsius (C), first subtract 32, then multiply by ⅝.
To convert from degrees Celsius to degrees Fahrenheit, multiply by ⅝, then add 32.

The color, materials, and detailing of this ramada make it a definitive example of this category. Round log posts team up with rough-sawn and roughly carved timbers, and the color is classic Southwestern. The Native American ladder adds another touch of authenticity.

 # Glossary

Beam. A large horizontal support member in a structure. See also girder.

Cantilever. A projecting beam that is supported at one end and at some midpoint along its length, with the other end extending into the air as if floating.

Casing. The wood trim or moldings that surround a door or window opening.

Conduit. Rigid or flexible tubing, made of metal or plastic, through which wires and cables are run. Often buried underground when used to convey electrical wire to an outdoor fixture.

Control joint. A narrow groove cut or tooled into a concrete slab to prevent random cracking from shrinkage or stress. Depth is usually about one-fourth of the slab thickness, and joints are usually cut to form square proportions in the slab sections.

Flashing. Thin metal barriers or layers, often preformed into bent shapes, used to divert water away from window and door openings and other interruptions in an exterior wall.

Footing. A thick concrete support for walls and other structures; buried below the frost line to prevent heaving when the soil freezes.

Frost heave. The lifting of a concrete slab or other structure from soil expansion due to freezing.

Frostline. The maximum depth frost penetrates the soil during winter.

This varies by region, and determines the necessary depth for deck piers, foundations, and post footings.

Girder (also girt). A timber-framing term sometimes used in association with pergolas and other open-frame structures. Typically, these are large beams that connect posts or sill plates to one another.

Glulam. Industry shorthand for glued-and-laminated, this term refers to large structural members (usually beams) that are made by laminating multiple layers of thinner boards into a single timber. Especially useful for curved components.

Ground-fault circuit interrupter (GFCI). An electrical safety device that senses shock hazards and automatically shuts off an electrical circuit. A GFCI can be a circuit breaker in the main panel or a special receptacle used in a kitchen, bathroom, or exterior setting.

Header. The beam that spans the top of a door opening or window opening.

Joist. A horizontal framing member, sets on its edge and spanning an open space below, that supports a floor or ceiling.

Knee-brace. A diagonal reinforcing member often used to strengthen the connection between a post and beam.

Ledger. A horizontal framing member fastened to a wall in order to support a floor frame or the joists in a deck structure.

Mortise-and-Tenon. A traditional woodworking joint that consists of a square or rectangular opening (mortise) cut into one part, which accepts a tongue (tenon) machined on a connecting part.

Nominal dimension. The stated dimensions of lumber or masonry components. In lumber, the nominal size reflects a roughsawn product, so the dimensioned piece is smaller. Likewise in masonry units, the nominal size includes the mortar joint, so the brick or block alone is slightly smaller than stated.

On-center. The term used to designate the distance from the center of one regularly spaced framing member to another, often kept uniform to allow for sheathing joints. Typical spacing is 16 inches for wall studs, floor joists, and rafters.

Pier. An individual/isolated masonry pedestal that supports deck posts and other structural components. Usually set atop or cast as an integral part of a poured concrete footing.

Pressure-treated wood. Lumber (typically southern yellow pine) that has been saturated with preservative compounds that resist insects and fungal decay. It is used for deck structures, sill plates, and other outdoor applications.

Setback. The distance from the edge of a structure to an adjacent property line, usually stated as a minimum requirement.

Substrate. A foundation layer of material upon with another material is installed or fastened.

⬛ Index

A

Akebia, five-leaf, 215
Arbors, 78–125
  about, 19, 80–85
  apertures in, 110–111
  Arts and Crafts-style, 11
  Asian-inspired, 82, 94–97
  classic, building, 86–89
  costs, 49
  curved-top, 118–121
  designing, 10
  with fences, 19, 108–109
  as front entries, 102–105
  with gates, 85, 90–93
  from kits, 43
  metal, 34–35
  on pedestals, 116–117
  for privacy, 19
  rustic, 98, 122–125
  with seating, 98–101
  tunnel, 112–115
Arches
  bentwood laminate, 120
  stack laminate, 118–119
Arts and Crafts-style structures
  arbors, 11
  pergolas, 13, 15
Asian-style structures
  arbors, 82, 94–97
  pergolas, 151
  for slopes, 22
  teahouses, 192–193
  trellises, 62

B

Bamboo, as building material, 33, 70–71
Bittersweet, American, 214
Bougainvillea, 214
Brick, as building material, 24, 28, 30
Budgeting, time and money, 48–49
Building codes, 46, 197
Building contracts, types, 48

C

Cantilevered construction, 23
Cedar, western red (lumber), 28
Clematis, 214
Climate
  average minimum temperature map, 219
  planning for winter appeal, 27
Color
  design role, 10, 12, 14–15, 84, 94
  paints, 40–41
Concrete
  as building material, 30
  construction techniques, 44
  for foundations, 24–25, 42
Construction techniques
  arbors, 87, 97
  arches, 118–120
  bamboo trellis, 71
  circles in trellis, 57
  circular apertures, 111
  concrete and masonry, 44
  copper tubing, 75
  cutting decorative edges, 89
  cutting tenons, 88
  finish work, 44
  gang-cut notches, 89
  gazebo kits, 170–171
  joining timbers, 45
  live-branch construction, 124–125
  masonry pedestals, 117
  overall assembly, 44
  pergolas, 133, 143, 151
  primer, 44
  screen-making, 190
  for slopes, 22–23
  tools, 44
  trellis mounting, 54
Contractors, working with, 44, 47
Copper, as building material, 33, 74–75
Craftsman-style structures
  arbors, 11
  pergolas, 13, 15

D

Decks
  with gazebos, 166–167
  with pergolas, 138–141
  privacy for, 19
Decorative edges, how to cut, 89
Designers, professional, 12
Designing structures, 8–49
  choosing materials, 28–37
  compatibility with home, 11, 14–15, 83, 102
  dos and don'ts, 13
  lighting, 26
  site selection, 20–25
  for winter interest, 27

E

Entries, 198–201
  front, arbors as, 102–105
  porches, 166–167
  rustic-style, 211
  See also Porticos

F

Fabric, adding to structures, 194–195
Fasteners and hardware, 37
Fences
  arbors with, 19, 108–109
  pergolas with, 146–147
Finishes. See Paints and finishes
Fireplaces, 196–197
Foundations
  anchoring posts, 25
  brick or concrete pavers, 24
  concrete slabs, 24
  for slopes, 23

G

Gang-cut notches, how to make, 89
Gates, arbors with, 85, 90–93
Gazebos, 158–177
  about, 16, 160–163
  construction, 168–171
  costs, 48–49
  for decks and porches, 166–167
  designing, 27
  from kits, 42, 164–165, 170–171
  roofs for, 172–175
  rustic, 176–177

H

Hardware and fasteners, 37
Honeysuckle, 216

I

Ipe (lumber), 28

J

Jasmine, common, 216
Jasmine, star, 216
Jessamine, Carolina, 216
Joinery techniques, 45

K

Kitchens, outdoor, 154–155
Kits
  about, 42–43
  costs, 42, 49
  for gazebos, 42, 164–165

L

Landscaping, 18, 44
Lath houses, 12, 20, 202–203
Lighting options, 26–27
Live-branch construction
  arbors, 122–123
  gazebos, 176
  materials for, 30
  pergolas, 32, 156–157
  techniques, 122–125
Lumber
  pros and cons, 28
  rough-sawn, 30
  selecting, 28

M

Mandevilla, 216
Masonry, construction techniques, 44
  See also Concrete
Materials, selecting, 14, 28–37
  See also specific materials
Mesh and wire building materials, 36, 190
Metallic building materials, 28, 34–35
  copper, 33, 74–75
  salvage and vintage, 33, 36
  wire and mesh, 36, 190
Metric conversions, 219

O

Obelisks and tuteurs, 72–73

P

Paints and finishes
colored, 40–41
finishes, 38–39
paints, 41
Passionflower, 217
Pavilions, 178–185
about, 180–185
rustic, 31
Pedestals
for arbors, 116
masonry, building, 117
Pergolas, 126–157
about, 126–131
above doorways, 142–143
Arts and Crafts-style, 13, 15
Asian-style, 151
attached, 134–137
benefits, 17
classic, building, 132–133
corner, 148–149
costs, 49
with curved tops, 150–151
with decks or patios, 16–17, 138–141
designing, 11, 13–14, 21, 29
for dining, 152–153
with fences or trellises, 146–147
freestanding, 144–145
with outdoor kitchens, 154–155
rustic, 32, 156–157
Victorian-style, 14
Pier footings
for kit buildings, 42
offset, for slopes, 23
post anchoring techniques, 25
Pine, pressure-treated, 28
Pool houses, 197
Porches, with gazebos, 166–167
Porticos, 15, 25, 198–201
See also Entries
Posts, how to anchor, 25
Privacy, structures for, 17–19, 66–69
Pyracantha, 217

R

Ramadas, 186–187
Redwood (lumber), 28
Roses, 215
Rustic-style structures
arbors, 98, 122–125
entrances, 211
gazebos, 176–177
pergolas, 156–157
rough-sawn lumber, 30
trellises, 53
See also Live-branch construction

S

Salvage and vintage building materials, 33, 36
Screened spaces, 18, 188–191
Screens, techniques for making, 36, 190
Seating
arbors with, 98–101
decks with, 19
Shade, structures for, 17
Shrubs or trees, for privacy, 18
Side yard solutions, 204–209
Silver lace vine, 217
Site preparation, 24–25, 42, 44
Site selection, 20–23
Slopes, building on, 22–23
Southwestern-style structures
arbors, 83
pergolas, 130
ramadas, 186–187
Stone, as building material, 28, 30

T

Tea ceremony, 193
Teahouses, 192–193
Temperature, average minimum, 219
Tenons, how to cut, 88
Terracing for slopes, 23
Tools, overview, 44
Trellises, 50–77
about, 52–54
Asian-inspired, 62
bamboo, building, 70–71
with circles, 56–57
copper, 33, 74–75
costs, 49
with curved tops, 58–59
from found or repurposed materials, 76–77
freestanding, 49, 62–65
from kits, 42
live-branch, 53
with pergolas, 147
for privacy, 18, 66–69
tuteurs and obelisks, 72–73
wall-mounted, 54–55, 60–61
Trumpet vine, 217
Tuteurs and obelisks, 72–73, 75

V

Victorian-style pergolas, 14
Vines
about, 18, 212
annual, 218
climbing techniques, 213
fragrant, 218
gallery of, 214–217
plants to avoid, 218
for tunnel arbors, 114

W

Whimsical structures, 210–211
Winter appeal, 27
Wire and mesh building materials, 36, 190
Wisteria, 217
Wood. See Live-branch construction;
Lumber

Large and exquisitely detailed, this ornate trellis is designed to stand as a formal architectural complement to a stately brick home. Weathered brick like this is never lacking in character, but such a large expanse calls for some visual relief, which the trellis provides.

Welcome Home

DECK & PATIO [*Design Guide*]

IDEAS & HOW-TO
Stone Landscaping
Paths · Steps · Patios · Walls

IDEAS & HOW-TO
Outdoor Kitchens
Planning · Grills · Fireplaces · Lighting · Hot Trends

Expert **advice** + **inspiration** + **ideas** + **how-to** for designing, building, maintaining your home's beautiful exterior